Manifesting Prosperity:
A Wealth Magic Anthology

Manifesting Prosperity: A Wealth Magic Anthology

Edited By
Taylor Ellwood

Manifesting Prosperity: A Wealth Magic Anthology
First Edition © Individual Contributors 2008

Cover by Andy Bigwood
Art Direction and Typesetting by Taylor Ellwood
Editor: Taylor Ellwood

Set in Poor Richard and Garamond

First Edition by Megalithica Books 2008

0 9 8 7 6 5 4 3 2

An Immanion Press Edition
http://www.immanion-press.com
info@immanion-press.com

8 Rowley Grove
Stafford ST17 9BJ
UK

ISBN 978-1-905713-15-8

Dedication:

This book is dedicated to every person who believes in opportunity. When you hear her knock, follow and who knows where you'll be.

Acknowledgments:

I would like to acknowledge the efforts of each contributor to this anthology to write articles on a subject that is often ignored in neopaganism and occultism. I am honored that each contributor chose to offer writing on this subject. I would also like to acknowledge Nicholas Pell's work as the copy-editor for this anthology. Finally, I appreciate the staff of Immanion Press/Megalithica Books, all of who have helped this book manifest so that it can help others manifest their own prosperity.

Table of Contents

Introduction

Manifesting prosperity is something that I believe most, if not all, people want. What prosperity is to you is probably different than what it is to me, but regardless of that, the desire to manifest prosperity is a primal force which expresses itself most in the desire to acquire pieces of paper and little round metal circles which is commonly called money. Plastic cards are also the rage, because they provide credit for the use of that money. Unfortunately people forget an important axiom that should always be remembered when it comes to manifesting prosperity into your life: **Money is not an end, in and of itself; it is a means to an end**. In other words, you can have lots of money and still not be prosperous. Money can enable you to manifest prosperity, provided you know what to do with that money. Having money, in and of itself, does little for someone who doesn't use it to enrich hir life.

This anthology provides techniques on how magic can be applied to help you manifest prosperity, particularly through such financial resources as money and credit. However, an even more important focus is the examination of personal responsibility and choices when it comes to managing your financial prosperity. I firmly believe that the personal choices we make set the tone for the wealth that we manifest in our lives.

There are some who will disagree. I've been told that it's not personal choices which cause people to be poor, but rather its broad economic trends which show that the rich keep getting richer and the poor keep getting poorer. However, I think claims like these are sometimes used as a justification for the circumstances that people find themselves in. Let me be clear and note that there are situations, such as life threatening illnesses, which can in fact devastate any financial reserve a person has. And it's certainly true that the wages paid to many people are wages that are pretty poor. The broken health care system and also the economic trends which can devastate a housing market or the credit market certainly impact jobs, which are usually the prime source of income for most people.

Nonetheless, even these factors can be mitigated by making responsible personal choices for finances. And while we may not have control of those broad economic trends, we do have control of our personal choices as well as of the attitude that we choose to take on when handling financial matters. People who argue that they are poor because of broad economic trends have chosen to give away any sense of empowerment when it comes to handling money because they believe it's too big for them to handle. They want to blame everything but themselves for the state of their financial being. People who are well off and argue that broad economic trends are the problem are people, who no matter how well intentioned, are inadvertently oppressing the very people they think they are helping. When you tell someone that they can't help the circumstances they are in, you take away the impetus to change those circumstances.

Financial wealth, and for that matter prosperity in general begins with personal choices. For example you can choose to take responsibility for your attitudes toward money, or you can continue to blame those broad economic trends for why you continue to handle money poorly. The choice is yours! In fact, the choice to be responsible for how you handle money is an act of magic, in its own way. Practical magic is based, after all, on the desire to change certain circumstances in your environment, or within yourself, in order to manifest a better alternative. By choosing to be responsible for how you handle money, you can also choose methods that can help you accomplish that goal. Magic is one of those methods.

Another method involves acquiring knowledge and understanding of the system you are working magic in. Finance is a system, and to really be empowered to manifest prosperity into your life, you have to understand how that system works. Many people get discouraged, believing that learning about finances is both stressful and dull, but if anything learning about finances can be fun, provided you have the right attitude and a desire to learn. The peril of ignorance isn't just credit card debt or even dealing with those broad economic trends I mentioned above. Rather, such ignorance can lead to living a lifestyle that you feel trapped in, because you need to pay off that mortgage or acquire lots of stuff, or whatever else it is you feel trapped about.

Understanding how finances work can lead to making informed choices, based off an awareness of what your circumstances, needs, and wants are. When you know how a system works you can manipulate that system and also apply other forces such as magic to it, in order to make it work for you, instead of against you. As a personal example, I am not sure I will ever buy a house. In the U.S. culture we are taught that buying a house is part of manifesting the American dream and also part of acquiring a source of wealth that builds up capitol, and yet with the sub-prime bubble popping this is clearly not the case. Even sources of finance that aren't associated with real estate have been impacted by the sub-prime bubble popping (one of those broad economic trends mentioned above). People are losing money on the houses they have bought. Factor in the expenses needed to make repairs, buy housing insurance, and the property taxes that need to be paid and the question of whether a house is a solid investment has to be reconsidered carefully in light of any other choices you may want to make. My desire, for instance, to manifest a successful independent business involves understanding that if I need to pay for a house and that business isn't initially as successful as it would need to be, to pay for that house, I might have to work at a regular job to pay for the house and thus delay my financial independence that much longer. The choices you make have an impact on the life you live. So, it's important to recognize that while you are impacted by broad economic trends, you are even more so impacted by your understanding of the financial systems you deal with and the choices you make based off that understanding.

In this anthology, it is our goal to show examples of wealth magic and explain how the techniques work. We also want to show where failures or shortcomings were encountered and how the practitioner refined the magic to address those shortcomings. Magic is a process, and when applied to any system there will be some successes, but also some failures. As long as we can learn and adapt we can eventually succeed in manifesting the prosperity we desire. The one thing we must not do is abdicate personal responsibility for our choices by claiming the reason we're poor is because of broad economic trends. Recognize those trends and recognize their impact, but also recognize your responsibility in making choices with how you manage your finances. No matter what financial "class" you fall into, you can still prosper, provided you understand the systems you're dealing with and effectively manage the resources you currently do have access to. A little magic to make situations go your way doesn't hurt either.

I can't guarantee that you will become fabulously rich if you read this anthology. I can say however that you may come away with a better awareness of how your choices and the attitudes that inform those choices can impact the financial wealth you do manifest in your life. I can also say that you may come away with a better sense of the options you do have access to. What you do with that awareness is what will determine if you can manifest the prosperity you desire into your life.

On a final note, I have created a LiveJournal community called PaganFinance[1]. This anthology is a complement to that community, and I encourage all of you to check it out. The goal of that community is to help each other learn how to handle finances better, and share our successes and failures so that everyone can benefit. By cooperating, instead of competing, we can manifest the prosperity that all of us deserve.

Taylor Ellwood
October 2007
Portland, OR

---

[1] http://community.livejournal.com/paganfinance

Undoing the Poor Occultist/Pagan Stereotype

Undoing The "Poor Pagan" Stereotype
By Taylor Ellwood

Ever heard of the stereotypical "poor Pagan"? The one who barely lives paycheck to paycheck, drives a hunk o' junk around because s/he has no credit, and never seems to get ahead? This stereotype, when it comes to money, is justified by the idea that being poor is virtuous. The rationalization is that it's okay if you're in debt, and/or don't have much money--you're keeping it real by not being too materialistic or capitalistic. Coyle sums up this stereotype best when she says, "I hated money because I hated what I saw as a mechanism of control and oppression. Poverty itself became a status symbol to show my friends" (2004, p. 196). But this virtue of being poor isn't really a virtue at all or a status symbol. For many (but not all), it's a rationalization for why a person is poor, so that s/he can feel better about hir decision to stay poor. Pagans aren't alone in this, but it seems that we are pretty good at providing reasons for accepting poverty over wealth. For those Pagans who are disabled or chronically ill, poverty may not be a choice, but instead an unfortunate reality that can't be avoided. Even so I have a suggestion at the end of this article as to how we as a community can help the members of our community who aren't as well-off because of situations radically out of their control.

While you may not have complete control over how much you're paid at a job[2], or the environment that you live[3], you can decide what you choose to do with your money. Even the debts you pay were debts that you took on, whether it was to purchase luxury items on a credit card or to deal with an unfortunate situation such as a car accident. Money management is an essential skill that many people lack for a simple reason. They have a bad attitude or bad conditioning about handling money and don't want to deal with it as a reality. What

---

[2] Though you may improve how much you're paid by continually performing excellent work, or by looking for a better job that pays what you're worth.

[3] Though this can be changed by either moving away or alternatively choosing to do what you can to improve the environment you live in (i.e. make sure your streets and sidewalks are litter free). The more you take care of your environment, the better chance that others will start to care as well.

this means is that when it comes time to pay bills or handle other financial situations they may be subconsciously sabotaging themselves and handling money in a way that's counter-productive.

You can take control of your attitude when it comes to money-- but you might not learn you have that control until after you're knee deep in debt and sinking further. In addition to the attitude problem that many people face (not just Pagans), another problem is that people aren't educated in financial literacy, i.e. how money works. High schools generally don't teach many classes on finances and other real-world issues and unless you decide to take courses in college about accounting or other related majors you likely won't get the education there. At home, unless your parents talk to you about money and how they handle it you likely will only learn how they handle it from observation. (And, of course, if your parents don't handle money well, chances are you won't either if you use them as examples!). Most of us learn what not to do with money, and that through hard experience, which is the absolute worst way to learn about finances.

You usually have to make costly mistakes to learn how to manage money effectively. Run up some credit card bills and you're stuck with high interest rates and struggling to pay the debt off. Don't put money away into savings or investments and you may find yourself working a fast food job in your eighties. Spend too much on books, video games, and other luxuries and you may not have enough money for the bills, therefore accumulating even more debt. Live paycheck to paycheck and when something big comes along, such as the transmission going out on your car, or an uninsured medical emergency, you're not going to have any way to pay for it. None of those experiences strikes me as particularly virtuous or desired.

Pagans and magicians don't have to be poor. I suggest, in fact, that we adopt the attitude that having money is a good thing. Money is good to have because it can insure relative self-sufficiency, and it can pay for unexpected situations, such as an accident or sickness. Money can pay for education and provide security for old age, and it can allow you to travel to other countries and experience other cultures at their source. Of course, those are just a few reasons why having money is good; I'm sure you can think of plenty of others.

We first need to look at our current attitude toward money. Take a moment and look at a bill or a checkbook or something else that's financially relevant. Take a pen in your hand and on a blank piece of paper write down your initial impressions when you look at the financial artifact and think of your monetary situation. If you find yourself writing and/or thinking of money in negative terms then you need to adjust your attitude. The reason you need to adjust it is because your attitude about finances is sabotaging the conscious choices you make when you have money. In fact, your attitude probably is one of scarcity, with worry focused on what you don't have. When the attitude is focused on what you don't have, you sabotage what you do have in an attempt to get what you don't have.

Because most people haven't been taught financial literacy we usually have negative experiences with money. This negativity imprints and we soon regard money as an affliction or a problem as opposed to a means of offering potential security and/or freedom from bad circumstances. Certainly this was the case for me, once upon a time. I always had some form of debt that needed to be paid off and yet no matter how I tried I just couldn't seem to get ahead or feel confident that my money would last beyond the current paycheck. But one day, having complained about money for the umpteenth time, I happened to pick up a book *Rich Dad, Poor Dad: What the Rich Teach their Kids About Money--That the Poor and Middle Class Do Not!* by Robert Kiyosaki. The core concept I got from this book was that I alone was responsible for how I spent my money and that my education about money and how I thought and felt about it greatly shaped my spending of it (Kiyosaki 2002). This seems like such an obvious point, but to someone who felt that money was an amorphous force that controlled his life, I found it to be liberating. No longer did money control me. Instead I could take control of it.

I suspect that many other magicians & pagans, were they to examine their attitude about money, would come to a similar realization. Although this awareness is liberating, we still need to undo the negative attitudes we have. There are a couple of ways to start doing this and I've found both of them have really helped me get a handle on my financial situation.

Meditation, Magic, & Consciously Loving Money

My first solution involved meditation. I prefer using Taoist meditation practices that involve dissolving internal energetic blockages. These energetic blockages usually also have emotions, beliefs, and attitudes attached to them. By dissolving the blockages I can allow myself to feel those emotions, beliefs, and attitudes, and then consciously change them so that they no longer sabotage me (Frantzis 2002). However, any technique will do provided it allows you to enter into a state of mind where you are receptive to examining and changing your beliefs on a particular subject. The reason this is important is because our everyday mundane consciousness tends to operate on autopilot, which means we don't always examine why we are doing what we are doing. By being contemplative and reflective about the problem we can see it from a perspective outside our everyday tunnel vision. This in turn can lead to conscious change.

Once you've examined the attitude and decided you want to change it, you need to determine what you will change it into. For example, I changed my attitude of money from dislike into love of money. I decided that I would love money and in return invite it to love me. Using meditation, I changed my memories of bad experiences with money into positive experiences where I learned to love money. I visualized myself in the various moments where I'd gotten negative imprints about money. I then visualized myself changing the actual occurrences into ones that were more positive in terms of how I handled money and felt about it afterwards. Through these meditations I was able to undo the negative imprints and create more positive ones that helped me feel more comfortable with handling money.

To reinforce this positive attitude further I decided to create an entity that would encourage my wife Lupa and I to love money and become more knowledgeable about it. Lupa made a pouch out of blue leather (we associate the color with money). In the pouch we placed a couple of coins and other personal effects that represented our desire to change our attitude and approach to money. I then came up with a phrase: "I love money". I took out the repeating letters, condensing the phrase into "Ilvmny", which was now the name of the entity. To bring the entity to life we decided that the energy that would feed it would be both the spending and receiving of money. Every transaction would give the entity energy to perform its task, which was to help us cultivate better financial habits. Our first transaction was to go out and buy books on money management. After each purchase and every time we make a sale, deposit a check, or invest in stocks we hold the pouch and say, "Thank you Ilvmny."

Although my first solution was to use magic to help me change my attitude, I also knew I needed to learn more about money. It wasn't enough to have a positive attitude about it. Something I've noticed in myself and many other people, Pagan and otherwise, is a decided lack of knowledge of how money works. Living from paycheck to paycheck illustrates this because it involves using money strictly for day to day survival with little preparation for the future. My second solution was to acquire financial literacy.

Financial Literacy: Making Money Work for You

I have a confession to make. When I created "Ilvmny" I figured all my problems were solved. I now had a wealth entity that would generate lots of money for me and everything would be okay. I had changed my attitude about money as well, so I figured that would be enough. But I was in for a surprise, because the entity asked me a question: "What do you know about handling the money you bring in?" I had to admit that I could handle my day to day finances, but beyond that, I wasn't sure. I didn't know the first thing about a retirement fund, or how to invest stocks. "Ilvmny" pointed out that it couldn't help me generate wealth if I didn't know much about how to handle or even how different financial systems worked. The reality of my situation was that I was living paycheck to paycheck.

When you live paycheck to paycheck you're working for money. This is what seems to happen to a lot of people. We go to work, we make money and we spend it, putting little, if any, aside for a rainy day or retirement. When a situation does come up we wish we had more money to solve it, even though it's not really more money that will solve the problem — it's making money work for you.

First, you need to learn how money works. If no one talked with you about money and how to use it responsibly then what you need to do is educate yourself. This doesn't have to involve evening classes at a college (and in fact that would probably be the most expensive and least successful way to learn about money in the immediate real world). Instead, I'd suggest going to your local bookstore or library and looking in the business and finance section. You'll probably want to get several books on how to handle personal finances because you never want to get just one person's opinion on any situation, let alone on how to handle money. I'll list a few recommendations at the end of this article, but you might also want to see what members of your family or friends have read about personal finances. Speaking of family, if you have kids, start talking to them about money as you learn. You can never educate your children about money too early. In fact, you may help them avoid mistakes you made and come out ahead when it comes to retirement and other financial matters.

Many people don't pick up books on money because they think such books will be loaded with technical financial jargon and hard to read. But a good book will explain the different terms and principles in a clear and concise manner. People also might think that money management is boring. While it may not be as riveting as, say, a mystery novel, once have a basic understanding you may find that it's actually an interesting subject to learn about. Even if you still don't find the subject fascinating, it's important to educate yourself about it. You don't need to know the intricacies of the daily life of a stock broker, but knowing the basics of how money works and how you can make it work for you will make your life a lot less stressful.

Making money work for you means learning how to invest in stocks and IRAs, maximize your 401k plan, and getting the most out of your bank accounts. When you know how to make money work for you, it becomes its own magic, with the result being more numbers than you had before, provided you take advantage of the systems in place. For instance, with stock investment, you don't have to invest stocks through a broker. You can invest in a company directly by taking advantage of the direct purchasing program offered through a company's dividend reinvestment program. This allows you to make your money work for you and know where that money is going. At the same time the wealth that is generated isn't wealth you had to earn. Instead you let other people (i.e. the employees in the company) earn it for you. To use another example of making money work for you, there's a lot more to a bank than free checking or savings. Do you know the interest rates of your account? Do you know the other options available to you at a bank? Do you know the differences between a bank and a credit union? Knowing the answers to those questions can impact how much your money works for you as opposed to you working for it[4].

Ideally, when money works for you, you have money to pay your bills, some set aside in savings to take care of emergency situations and some applied toward investments for your eventual retirement. You want your money to grow in such a way that a lot of the money you make isn't even money you had to work for. Your goal isn't necessarily to end up rich (though that doesn't hurt) but it is to end up financially secure, without having to worry how you'll pay off your debt or take a day off work without pay or even retire. If you do want end up really rich, you may have to take some big risks to get there.

As you learn financial literacy, you'll develop your own style of managing your resources, as well as determining how to achieve your goals. The reason you want to read a variety of authors on this subject is so you can get some different perspectives on how money is

---

[4] If you don't know the answers I'll leave it to you to do some research. It's worth your time, trust me.

managed and grown. You likely won't agree completely with each perspective, but you'll get something out all of them. The most important thing to do though is not to rush. Read, research, and decide what will work best for you when it comes to managing your money. If you can, play a game that simulates financial situations, before actually committing yourself. Playing such a game lets you take some risks without losing any money. A game I'd recommend is Virtual Stock Exchange, which lets you invest in stocks in a simulated stock market[5].

Are We Getting Too Materialistic?

I suggested earlier that the poor Pagan stereotype is not virtuous, for the simple fact that being in debt and/or having to worry whether you'll make your ends meet each week or month is never an ideal place for anyone to be in. But is having money evil? I think, in and of itself, money isn't good, evil, or any other moral value we may place on it. It is however a force, one that must be acknowledged and respected because it's one we interact with everyday. Even learning how money works won't necessarily make you more or less materialistic, though it will help you become better informed about your spending habits.

Where the virtue (or lack thereof) comes in is with you and your choices. Once you know what your spending habits are you can choose to change them. If you find yourself spending most of your money on luxury items for yourself, perhaps it's time to stop purchasing them. Find other uses for your money such as your child's college fund or funding for that trip to Europe you've always wanted to take, but never had enough time or money for. Or you could simply choose to be more generous with your money.

Another stereotype that Pagans are accused of is of not offering enough public services or charities that help the community at large. As Pagans become more successful with money this perception can be changed. When you have more money to spare you can put some of it toward the charity or public service of your choice. Better yet, you can help those members in your community who are poor and have no choice in it. Adopt a Pagan family or person who's less well off. Donate money or food or other goods to help them out. Support your community and in doing so create a closer connection so that everyone can benefit. Remember though that money alone won't solve the world's problems or even that of a local community. Devoting

---

[5] http://www.virtualstockexchange.com/Game/Homepage.aspx

some time to public service or giving some food to food banks or doing some other form of community work is equally valuable and worth doing.

Loving money doesn't mean you're a materialist and out to steal from the poor. Loving money merely means that you enjoy being prosperous and prefer it over other circumstances. You won't turn into a yuppie or a snob by choosing to love money, unless you want to. For me, loving money isn't about putting money before everything else; it's really loving the idea that I don't have to worry if I'll be able to pay this or that bill or feel guilty because I wanted to buy the latest Jim Butcher novel. There's enough to worry about in life. Security about money or bills or buying a book without cleaning out your checking account is something all of us can have provided we accept that having money doesn't equal being materialist. Remember, it's your choices that define how you think of yourself and who you are.

I recently created a shrine for my wealth entity. It's not to worship money, but it is to show respect for it, and its place in my life. The pouch that represents the physical entity was placed beside a small coin bank I have. The coin bank is actually a small armor truck with four cylinders for each type of coin. A sigil is painted on the truck to attract more coins to it. Every time I come home with change, the change is put into the cylinders and eventually wrapped up and deposited in my savings account. Above the bank truck and the pouch is a painting of a magical dollar bill. The shrine is a good reminder to respect the impact money has on my life and on the lives of people around me.

Money is a medium. Without it, we can't easily survive. With it we can enjoy what life offers while establishing financial security for the rough times and old age. Remember that it's not how much you make that insures a good relationship with money; it's how you use the money you do make that determines if you have a good relationship with it. Even someone who doesn't make a lot of money can still come out ahead by using the resources s/he has wisely. And you can always help other members in the community who aren't in as good a situation as you are. None of us have to be "poor Pagans".

Bibliography

Coyle, T. Thorn. (2004). *Evolutionary witchcraft.* New York: Penguin Books.
Frantzis, B. K. (2002). *Relaxing into Your Being: Breathing, Chi, and Dissolving the Ego.* Berkeley: North Atlantic Books.

Kiyosaki, Robert T. (2000). *Rich Dad, Poor Dad: What the Rich Teach Their Kids About Money--That the Poor and Middle Class Do Not!* New York: Warner Business Books.

Recommended Reading

The Motley Fool: You have more than you think by David and Tom Gardner
The Motley Fool Investment Guide by David and Tom Gardner
http://www.fool.com
The Intelligent Asset Allocator by William Bernstein
The Richest Man in Babylon by George S. Clason
Smart Couples Finish Rich: 9 Steps to Creating a Rich Future for You and Your Partner by David Bach
Secrets of the Millionaire Mind by T. Harv Eker

Wealth and Abundance
By Janet Callahan

In the coven I used to belong to much of the learning was self-directed; based on meetings with the High Priestess about how things were going in our lives and some questions she asked each of her students to see what areas of their lives each initiate needed to work on. When I was an initiate several years back, one area my High Priestess always asked about was the challenges that were going on in our lives. What came out of my discussion with her was an assignment to go work on manifesting abundance in my life.

It was a strange assignment, as far as I could tell. My husband and I have professional jobs. We have a house that was new when we bought it, in a quiet neighborhood, just a few blocks from an excellent elementary school, nice cars…more cars than drivers, in fact. We own a business, which is at a break-even point, plus or minus a bit – and when it's minus, we invest in the business from our personal accounts to make up the difference. We have more than three computers per person in our house, and more than one printer per person, along with all the other electronic toys you can name. Sure, we have debt, but doesn't everyone? And our debt was either from the business, or from stupid things we did in college when we didn't have jobs.

But I went home and tried to sort through why she'd made this assignment, because I respected her insights. Before I could even think about trying to manifest abundance, I needed to figure out why I should be thinking about it and what it meant to me. And so that's what I set off to do. Being an engineer, and having a much stronger affinity for research than for meditating, I started with the dictionary. Merriam-Webster says that abundance is "an ample quantity: PROFUSION," "AFFLUENCE, WEALTH," or "relative degree of plentifulness." That definition didn't seem to be all that helpful – I *have* an affluent lifestyle, I consider myself to be wealthy. I have many of the material things I want, and there are very few things that I might want that I couldn't buy, if I wanted to. I rarely do "prosperity" spells – quite honestly, money comes when I need it because I have a really good job, and so does my husband, and even when we weren't gainfully employed, manifesting money to pay the bills was never a problem, so why abundance?

Since I hadn't managed to research my way out of this problem, I realized I was going to have to meditate and look at my life, and figure out what things my High Priestess saw that I didn't. And over the course of several weeks, I realized that the *connotations* of abundance that had been instilled in my thoughts were where the real problem was.

In my exploration of my thoughts on money and abundance, I realized that I had been conditioned to believe that all I needed was to be able to pay this month's bills before they were due. Much reflection brought me to the realization that, in my mind, abundance really boils down to having enough money to pay the bills - and that's it. There's nothing there about having the money to get things without using plastic (because as long as the credit card bill is paid, you're good). Further, while I live a fairly material-rich lifestyle now what I began to realize was that there was so much more that I could have, if I could get beyond the conditioning of my childhood that just paying the bills was the only thing money was good for, and the only real goal.

I grew up in a lower middle class family. My parents hid the reality of our situation from us kids, but we knew money was an issue. We lived in a lower middle class neighborhood, where everyone went to yard sales to buy clothes, and where it wasn't uncommon for people to get food stamps when they lost their jobs, or to get free lunches at school all year round. Our moms traded coupons. At my house, my grandparents gave us canned fruits and vegetables from their garden, and they butchered meat for us too. And all of these experiences taught me that the best you could hope for, money wise was to work hard, only buy the necessities, and hope you had enough to pay all the bills.

When I went to my next review with my High Priestess, she asked what I had learned about abundance, and I told her about my feeling that I thought money meant being able to pay the bills, without necessarily having anything extra.

She asked if I'd thought beyond money in my meditations, and I realized that I hadn't. Time is another key player here; a lot of the things we did when I was a kid to make up for the lack of money took a *lot* of time. And a lot of the services I pay for now, like hiring a lawn service to mow the grass, are me spending money to gain more time. The two concepts are intrinsically linked.

When I asked her why abundance was the thing she wanted me to work on, she pointed out that one of the most stressful things in my life at that point had been that I felt that my house has been taken over, and I didn't know how to regain control.

At the time, our business, a non-profit group, and a fledgling temple were all being run out of my house. Also, my husband and I had two roommates – one who worked for us and came with two cats, and another was an old friend leaving a bad relationship, with three more cats, to go along with our three cats. We had been working on finding a building for the temple to turn into public ritual space (and a library, and a meditation room, and all those other things that Pagan organizations seem to need), and had manifested several really nice buildings that were perfect…we'd just not manifested a way to pay for any of them. The same was true for the business – the basement and garage were serviceable, but I really needed the mental space that getting it out of the house would provide, and the money to do so wasn't easily available. The non-profit needed an office and a part time office assistant so I'd have more time. And all of this needed to happen without me paying for it by creating more debt.

My High Priestess and I had a long discussion about the things I needed in my life. Beyond money, and time, things like good friends and love and spiritual fulfillment. And that sometimes, spending extra time could save you money, and sometimes spending a little money could save you time, but they're not necessarily interchangeable.

So, with that new understanding, she sent me home to try again. I started by deciding that I needed to re-define abundance in my mind. First, I started by making a list of what I think abundance should be in my new world view. And while it's not just money, it certainly starts there.

Defining Abundance for Myself

For me, having a life of abundance now includes:

* First and foremost, no debt. No credit card debt, no car loans, no student loans – the only allowed debt is the mortgage on our house. If I can't pay it off this month, I should set the money aside until we have enough to pay cash.
* Having money to travel without putting it on a credit card, and to be able to enjoy traveling without watching every penny or skipping some activities because they're too expensive.

* Having time to travel – not cutting trips to visit family or friends short because I don't have enough vacation days.
* Having money to deal with a large unexpected purchase in cash – car repairs, household appliances breaking down, and similar situations.
* Having money to go out for the evening when I want, including nice restaurants, the symphony, or concerts, rather than sticking with fast food and then going to the movies at the dollar show.
* Having time to spend with my spouse, and with good friends and other important people.
* Being able to save up money for things like improvements on the house or a new car, rather than putting those types of things on a credit card and paying them off later, or waiting for the tax refund.
* Building the business to the point where it can support itself, in a building other than my house, with several full time employees.
* Being able to make my living from my business and other outlets, rather than continuing to work for a large corporation.
* A rich social life with many friends, both locally and in other places, whom I can spend time with and enjoy being around.
* A rich family life - having children in particular, but also enjoying the time I have with my family.
* Having time to work on things that I personally find meaningful – writing, reading, meditation, magick, and the like.
* Giving myself time (and motivation) to treat myself better, in body, mind and spirit.
* Being able to treat myself to things like massages and manicures, and to join a gym or take a dance class without feeling like I am short-changing the family budget.
* Making sure that the organizations that I am involved with having everything they need, while maintaining a balance between my needs and the organizations' needs.
* Learning when to say no – both in terms of my time and my money – when I can't take on something new, and when to let go of things that aren't working. And allowing myself the mental space to know that this is not a character flaw.

Taking Control of the Abundance in My Life

The next step was to gain control of the household budget. Every expense is now tracked in a software program, by category. All expenditures above about $20 are discussed between my husband and I before they are made.

One of the key points that I realized in doing this was that if I had no credit card debt, I wouldn't need credit cards – a fairly sizeable portion of our income goes to pay those bills, and only major expenses go on them these days. Even more, though, was the realization that, without debt, my husband or I could decide to quit our day jobs to focus on our business, without sacrificing much (if any) of the comfortable life we have now. So we made a plan to start focusing on paying things off now, delaying purchasing any new things that aren't essential, and putting some money aside in savings.

Next came the mental work to do some internal transformation to help make this all a reality. I set about building a picture in my mind of how life would be if I had these things. Our house would have me, my husband, our cats, and eventually our children. We'd be able to park a car in our two-car garage, rather than having the garage full of a roommate's furniture and all the extra storage for the business. We'd have a large building a short drive away, housing our business, the non-profit organization's office, and a meditation space for the temple. I'd work there, bouncing between the business, work needed by the other groups sharing the building, and writing on my own, as time and work load dictated. I'd be able to keep a schedule based on what makes my body happiest, rather than based on my employer's preferred work hours. When we do have children, we'd set up a room just for the kids in that building housing the business, and run our own little mini-daycare for our employees.

Every week in my own private rituals, I would raise energy around this vision, making it feel more and more real each time. I took a Chinese coin and charged it with this energy, and I carry that coin around in my wallet to this day. Every time I open my wallet, I see that coin and am reminded to think before spending money, and particularly before pulling out a credit card. I'm reminded of where we're going, and where we've been.

I wrote up a very detailed list of all the things I needed to have happen – the office, more business, both of our then-current roommates moving out, all of it. And I asked my coven for help – in fact, they decided to make helping me manifest it all the major working during one full moon ritual.

Within a month, one of our roommates had moved out.

Even more important, though, was re-programming all the things that told me this was not abundance – the things that made my relationship with money dysfunctional. Many people would go back and re-live experiences, changing things along the way, replacing the old memories with better ones. But in this case, I thought a different tactic was in order.

Over the course of several months, I went memory by memory through all the lessons on wealth and abundance in my childhood. And I firmly planted a "marker" in my head for each one, where I could stand and watch both the way things were, and the way things could have been at the same time – like watching TV using the picture-in-picture feature. In each case, I left the old memory intact, but with a clear comparison of how things could have been, rather than how they actually were.

And now, every time I think about how I could do something the "old" way, I pull up those memories as a reminder – it could be so much better if I stick to the new way of acting. I also routinely set up both "versions" of any potential decision, and compare the likely results as a way of making sure I stay on the right path.

Moving Forward With Abundance

It's a long journey, and I've certainly not solved all the problems yet.

Money wise, we have been making progress - we've been paying our employee from the business account instead of our personal accounts more often than not, and business is picking up.

Only a handful of things have gone on the credit cards in the last year and a half – and most of them were unusual business purchases, not personal ones. We've re-arranged the credit cards, getting the interest rates down very low - and we've got a plan to have them all paid off in a few years.

The car loans got paid off, as have a couple of other outstanding loans, and we're focusing on throwing everything we have towards paying off one specific debt, then another. We've also got a savings account, with an automatic withdrawal from our regular account every paycheck.

This year we went on a short vacation, and paid for it all straight from our bank account. While our tax refund is going to pay for our new deck, there will be money left over for paying off other things, and for putting aside for emergencies.

We've spent some money organizing – the business is largely confined to the basement these days, and one of our walk-in closets (which has a window where I can see the moon) became my library and meditation room, with a small working altar.

Time wise, the temple got shut down due to it simply taking up too much time for too little reward. And the time saved there has been re-allocated to my friends and family.

The remaining roommate is working on moving out this year. While he's said that before, without much success, this time he has an actual plan to make it happen.

I found the non-profit group a tiny corner of someone else's office and hired an office assistant, and then three months later moved to a better office that meant having our own space. We've also been blessed with a handful of office volunteers who are working through a lot of the things that I just don't have time to do.

The combination of changes means that I have more time to write, and more time to hang out with people who are important to me. It means I have more energy to put towards ritual, and more money to put towards paying off bills. And with each bill that gets paid off, there is even more money to put towards paying off the other bills.

And over time, the things I used to do seem more and more alien to me. The new ways of viewing things seem more normal, and are easier to follow. It's been a long time since we went and bought something "just because" – both my husband and I are more likely to put off the initial desire for something until we've had time to discuss and determine whether we can pay for it in cash.

We've also decided to clean out closets and storage areas, have a yard sale, and donate whatever is left to charity. My husband started taking the bus to work because it was cheaper than driving, and in doing so, we have decided to sell one of the cars, and the motorcycle. They're nice status symbols, but just not really important to us anymore.

Even one of my most closely held desires – the desire not to let people down – has fallen to the strength of this new vision of how I want life to be. I came to the conclusion while writing this article that I would resign as director of the non-profit organization I've run for the last two years. The stress I was under to keep things functioning and the time it takes away from my family finally reached a point where they outweigh the good things that running the group brought me. While it is not the easiest thing for the organization to handle, I'm sure they'll find someone equally talented who will be able to do a fine job running it. In the meanwhile, the 20-30 hours a week that I've put into this the last two years will now be used for other things, particularly writing, growing the business, and spending time with the people who are important to me.

Because wealth is not about what you do, or how much you do, it's about what kind of life you live with what you've got.

Bibliography

Merriam Webster Online Dictionary, Retrieved July 9, 2007 from http://www.m-w.com/dictionary/abundance

Janet Callahan is a Detroit-area Pagan forging her own path as a Modern American Polytheist. Ms. Callahan wears a large number of hats, including Dianic priestess, writer, artist, business owner, and engineer, although she's recently permanently retired the hat that says "Program Director of SpiralScouts International." Ms. Callahan has previously had articles published in *Cup of Wonder* and has had poetry published on paganliving.com. As always, Ms. Callahan appreciates the unconditional love and never-ending support of her husband Barry, her mother Linda, and her close friends and family-by-choice, JCB and JTT, as she pursues a more creative and fulfilling life.

Financial Magic
Vincent Stevens, I.S.U.A.G.

A note on definitions:

In this essay, I use the term "financial magic" to refer to all magic working in the financial sphere from job hunting, to attracting money, to gaining wealth.

Introduction

I was introduced to complex financial magic in 2004, when I decided to apply my interest in magic to financial means. I had often avoided it for such purposes as most reports I had heard on financial magic had been of results that were at best unreliable or unpredictable or at worst complete failures or disasters. In addition, I had seen people often distracted by financial magic to the point that they failed to apply non-magical (and more effective) solutions to their issues.

However, as my magical practices had gone on, I became aware of the many ways one could apply magic, and that financial magic was an area that promised to be both helpful and interesting to explore. After having several definite successes in financial magic, I felt I can use this essay is an attempt to codify my findings and experience into a useful guide.

In talking to several pagans and magicians over the years, I have heard them decry the state of financial knowledge in the pagan and magical community. I have argued in turn that this is not a problem unique to any community. In my country, the United States - people's financial understanding is often abysmal and it's not relegated to any one group or subculture. As of this writing, I live in a country whose savings rate, for the population as a whole, border on the negative - and this during a time of changing economies and Globalization.

Financial knowledge is important to financial magic for one simple fact - if you don't understand the system you're working magic with and on, your magic's chance of success is much lower. What financial knowledge I have came, in fact, from realizing how much I and my friends didn't know when I was younger and sitting down and learning. In short, a good deal of my knowledge comes from a post-college panic where I realized the depths of my own ignorance. These moments are excellent teaching tools, so treasure your panic. People may know their gods, their Sephiroth, and their spells, but if you're working on something as a "black box" of a system that's a mystery to you, then you have less to work with. Your magic and its outcomes will be affected as you can't "connect" to the contents of what you're trying to work with. Magic is a useful tool. It is the ability to take the complex relations of the world and synchronize them with our mental and physical activities, and bring about effective results by this interaction. But if we don't understand the systems, including the financial systems we work with, we limit ourselves.

So, in short if you're going to do financial magic, you need to understand how the financial world works. That may sound boring, trite, or frightening, if not a combination of all three. However, I've found in both financial knowledge and financial magic, understanding finance can be an exciting experience. Money and trade have been with humanity since the beginning, and it is well worth getting to know them better.

The rest of this essay presents an outline for integrating financial knowledge into your magical practices. You may not do everything listed below; perhaps in fact you're in an emergency and need some financial magic now. But the exercises and time line below are meant to produce understanding, and results.

Step 1: Your Psychology Of Money

The first step to dealing with financial systems and magic is dealing with ourselves, our thoughts, and feelings about money. In fact, as you do financial magic, your own psychology will be with you for all of your practices - so you need to understand yourself first. After all, no matter how many magical models you use or gods you invoke, you yourself are still the one common factor to all your work, your successes, and your failures.

The problem with understanding our attitudes and psychological approaches to money is not ignorance - it's the fact that we're used to it. Purchasing, investing, and paying bills are all so automatic to us, so common that we don't think about them. We're swimming in a sea of electronic payments and exchanges of currencies, often little aware of what we're doing, why, and what it means - until we pause and think.

Making the effort to understand your attitudes towards financial issues lets you be a more effective magician. You can figure out how to direct your energies, how to work around any particular personal

34

issues that may sabotage your efforts, and avoid mistakes in the future. You may even learn a few related things you didn't expect, or have a good laugh at your past successes or mistakes.

I strongly recommend that, if you are new to financial magic or at all unsure of your goals and abilities, you review your attitudes and feelings about finance with the exercises below before making any attempt at workings. The psychology of money, economics, and finance is subtle and something we all too rarely think about. You don't need any backfire or even unexpected successes in such a delicate area. The wrong success can be as much of a problem as a failure or backfire.

These exercises are designed to make you pause - and think. Use them as recommended and as needed. They are not overtly magical, but may lead to useful discoveries. Your goal, in short, is to better understand yourself. You might be surprised how much you don't know about this person.

EXERCISE 1:

Write down five things you believe firmly about money, finances, or economics. Once you've written them down, ask yourself why you chose to believe them. Do not blame anyone or anything else; determine your choice, conscious or subconscious, for each thing. If you're not sure you can come up with an explanation, pick the best one that pops into your mind - its likely closer to the truth than you realize. Take complete responsibility for your beliefs.

Think over your answers and write down the impressions you had about yourself and your answers.

If you are determined to do financial magic, do this exercise at least once a week until you feel comfortable doing it. See what you learn about yourself and what you believe. What do you find out?

EXERCISE 2:

Write down your financial goals. Do this once a month as you engage in financial planning or magic. Again, ask yourself why you chose these goals and take complete responsibility for them. Keep this up during your financial magical practice.

This may be a good exercise for life. Consider making it a monthly or yearly exercise - I have had great success with regular reviews.

EXERCISE 3:

Take some quiet time, sit down, and review financial issues in your head - your retirement, your job, your bank account, etc. Observe your mental and physical reactions to thinking of these things - how do you feel mentally and physically, and what does this tell you about yourself? What do you wish to change about yourself regarding your reactions? This may be an opportunity to plan some psychological magic on yourself.

EXERCISE 4:

Write down all the changes you've seen in the financial world since you've been able to remember - recessions, innovations, crises, fads, and so forth. Review them and ask how they affected you and your life, and how they affected your attitudes. How did they affect the above exercises?

In doing these exercises you may reach points of feeling extreme emotions - shame, greed, confusion, self-loathing, intense happiness, etc. Though they may be unpleasant, make your best effort to stay with them - don't avoid them, but let yourself experience them fully. Learn what they tell you. Get to know them. Stand right in the center of the unpleasant feelings and live them for that time until they pass on their own.

In exploring your feelings about money, wealth, and finances, you can start cultivating a healthy understanding and relationship with them. When you feel you're ready to proceed, move on to stage 2.

Step 2: Understanding Finances And Financial Systems

Once you have assessed your psychology of money (or indeed, while you assess it, if you feel confident) it's time to work on your financial knowledge.

Financial education is an ever-continuing process (change is, as is said too often, the only constant) and that means economies, job markets, even the medium of exchange changes over time. As of this writing, debit cards are ubiquitous, but would have been unheard of some 30 years ago. The Euro was just a glimmer of imagination two decades ago. The world of finance evolves and doesn't show any sign of stopping.

So if you're going to do financial magic, get educated. Otherwise what are you exactly doing magic on? First, if you don't have basic financial knowledge, or aren't comfortable with it, get yourself a good primer on basic money management, investing, and retirement. The classic "Idiots" or "Dummies" books (despite the condescending titles) are good sources of starter information Classes at a local college or education center are also useful. If you aren't educated in basic financial management, get educated first and foremost.

There are a few techniques to engage in throughout your life to stay financially educated:

* Keep reading on financial issues as new books, publications, news shows, etc. come out.
* Get a subscription to a good financial magazine and read it when it comes in - don't feel you have to read every article, but learn to find ones useful to you and interesting to you. Keep each issue until the new one comes in.
* Watch the business news when you can, and read the business section of your paper - at least the Sunday edition.

As you increase your financial understanding, try the following exercises. Your goal is to understand finances better, and what may keep you from understanding them.

EXERCISE 1:

In pursuing financial education, what negative feelings and associations do you find? Why? Do these have any grounding in reality? Do they reveal anything more about what you found in the first set of exercises?

Some people are adverse to financial education. It can seem boring (and at times be boring). They may worry about becoming materialistic (which is a risk anyways). They may also worry about loosing touch with important realities and see things in financial abstractions (which can happen). What have you experienced?

EXERCISE 2:

For the next month, whenever you read financial or business news, take whatever story catches your attention each day or week, and write down what possible impact it could have on you. Even if it seems irrelevant, dig until you can find some logical impact, no matter how small.

EXERCISE 3:

Once every week or two, for at least two months, pick a financial phenomenon to study: it can be inflation, wage gaps, mutual funds, etc. Think over this phenomenon. Read up on it through books or web pages.

Go to whatever room you use for rituals and meditation, perform any warding or mind-clearing exercises, and put yourself into a meditative state. When you are relaxed, focus on the phenomena - what color would you associate with it? What sensations? What smells? Feel the phenomena in question as a colorful cloud of energy in the world. Feel how it affects you.

Now, feel how the phenomenon affects people you know. See the colorful energy you share with those people, for good or for ill. When you have a good sense of connection and understanding, move on to the next phenomenon.

Now, feel how it affects people in general. Again, feel the energy of the phenomena that you share with others, feel the connection. When you have a good sense of connection and understanding, move on to the next phenomenon.

Now, feel how the phenomenon affects non-human institutions such as traditions, banks, etc. When you have a good sense of connection, move on.

Now that you've done this analysis, ignore the people and institutions and traditions. Again, just feel the phenomena - its color, smell, sensations, etc. Feel and experience it without the associations or those it affects. Feel the phenomena itself as you perceive it.

Write down your experiences and keep a record of them. These associations will assist with your later work.

This is not a shamanic or contact exercise *per se*, but if you find yourself slipping into a trance, astral state, etc. you should ward and banish properly.

Step 3: Magical Exploration

Having broadened your self-knowledge and understanding of financial issues, its now time to explore the magical side of the issue. For those of you following these steps closely, this is when things finally get occult.

Financial issues, financial institutions, and financial phenomena aren't dead or simple things - they're alive and they're powerful. Anyone who's ever seen a major economic change, such as a recession or a boom, can see financial phenomena take on a living, even mythical quality. It's no small leap to see inflation as a devouring demon, or Hermes having a hand in the age of the Internet Economy. In your explorations in Step 1 and especially Step 2, you can start seeing the complexity of the financial world, a world that one can understand magically.

In fact, an examination of magical practices throughout history reveals that no small amount of these practices is of a "financial" nature. Hunting magic is about gaining game. There are treasure-seeking demons in the Goetia. The pursuit of gold led many people to take literally the mystical practices of alchemy. Charms, talismans, spells, and more are all available and documented repeatedly for the mage who needs a financial boost.

However, if you're going follow tradition and apply magic to financial situations, you need to know them magically. Spells and rituals are stale unless you have a feel for the issues, the symbols, and the principles involved.

You've gotten to know yourself. You've gotten to know financial principles and news in the world. So next up, with that foundation, it's time to get to know the magical side of finance with the following exercises.

EXERCISE 1A:

If you have any particularly favorite gods or pantheons you use in your work, pick the gods most relevant to financial issues (or ones you're interested in), and engage in a study of their symbols, history, and cultural associations. If you have done so before, review them, and do your best to push your studies further than before. Ask yourself:

* What their historical roles were, how they changed, and why?

* What their symbols are and how they were important to the culture(s) they were revered in?
* What rituals were associated with them, how were they performed?
* What were their personalities like?

This exercise can be very revealing. A small example from my own experiences is how many gods of prosperity started off as gods of agriculture. How one defines prosperity does affect how one pursues it...

Feel free to do this exercise multiple times.

EXERCISE 1B:

If you're prone to making your own god-forms, and 1A isn't your thing (or if it is and you want another exercise), go and create a new financial deity that is either general or focused on an issue important to you. Go all out and write down descriptions, associations, and whatever comes to you. Don't over think this, but let it be a straightforward artistic endeavor. When you're done:

* Look at the symbols, attributes, and associations of the new godform. Look them up in an appropriate reference (I recommend starting with Manfred Lurker's "Dictionary of Gods and Goddesses, Devils and Demons")
* Why did you give the god-form the personality traits you did? What associations do you have with these traits?
* What rituals would be best to invoke this god-form?

Feel free to do this exercise multiple times.

EXERCISE 2:

Now that you've gotten to know at least either a "classic" god or a new god-form, spend at least a week invoking the deity in question, making ablutions, praying/invoking for guidance and information, and looking for the deity's hand in the world. Record your dreams and any experiences. Continue this exercise as long as it takes for you to have a meaningful dream, contact, or experience. Engage in all usual magical cautions during this exercise.

EXERCISE 3:

This is a more complicated exercise. Select a god you've chosen, a god-form, or even one of the financial principles you explored in section 2. You're going to make a journey to understand it.

This is a far more serious exercise than above. Take your standard practice for any shamanic/astral/spirit world journey, including all of your precautions. When you're ready, use your preferred trance/journeying method and go and converse with the god, spirit, or the spirit of the financial principle you've chosen.

When you make contact do the following:

     *   Ask to better understand your chosen subject.
     *   Ask for advice on how to do better financial magic.
     *   Ask for any particular guidance you may need.

Be sure to close and banish appropriately. Write down and look over your experiences. What can you learn from them?

OPTIONAL EXERCISE:

Pick a major financial incident in the past. Depending on your magical persuasion, ask yourself which gods, demons, spirits, etc., was part of it. Consider invoking them for a better understanding of that phenomenon, or perhaps a banishing to protect yourself. Try this exercise several times if you'd like. You may not feel comfortable doing such work until you're further along your exercises.

Step 4: Your Financial Goals

You're ready for magic. You've analyzed, probed, visited, and visualized.

Not quite.

When doing financial magic, you need to have your financial goals in mind first. You can't do effective magic - or anything else - without an actual financial plan and goal in mind. Admittedly if you're using magic because of a crisis situation, long-term planning may not be worth focusing on in the immediate future. But if you have the breathing room, plan.

Establish good financial goals and strategies, even if those are learning more, taking a course, or getting a job to give you financial breathing room. Review them regularly. I recommend quarterly and annually. Any good financial advice book can help you out with this.

Leverage your psychological and magical findings from the above exercises in this case. This is where your magical work gives you a distinct edge. You've explored issues in intimate ways. You've got your Tarot cards or your yarrow sticks to get new ideas and solve issues. Leverage what you've found. But your financial plan is a financial plan first, not a magical outline per se.

And then, when you have your goals, when you know what you want to do - it's time for magic.

Step 5: Applied Financial Magic

That's the simplest part of the essay in a way. Take your financial plan, and determine where you can use magic to make it work. Magic is no different than any other financial tool in this case. You may need to modify your personality, banish a troublesome entity, or attract potential employers. Take the magic and run with it. You've got the understanding to be more effective.

If there's a problem in financial magic, I find it's deciding how specific one wants to be in one's workings. You can focus on a specific goal like getting a job at a given company, or a general goal like improving your financial opportunities. Be honest with yourself about the goal your setting. Don't fall into the trap of making every spell have intent so focused and narrow you ruin the chance that it could occur merely by piling so many conditions on it. Magic is open and alive (and so is the world of finance), so you'll need to play with the financial magic in a way that works.

I prefer to combine both methods. As of this writing I use talismanic magic to set a general mood for my household, use some general rituals to assist my financial understanding, then specific invocations for specific goals.

As for advice in rituals - that's the easy part. Any magic 101 book can give you a way to perform a ritual for anything or a way to construct a ritual on your own.

It's having the knowledge and background to make financial magic truly about financial issues that's important.

EXERCISE 1:

Pick one general financial situation you'd like to enhance or improve otherwise. Develop a ritual, spell, talisman, etc. for it. Spend at least one month, or longer if you determine it is necessary, to chart the results. Try altering your general financial situation bit by bit using this method.

EXERCISE 2:

Pick a series of specific financial goals to reach magically. Perform a spell for each one at a time. Do not start a new one until the other one played out or you are convinced of failure.

Using good financial magic is a skill all of its own. As much as we are told to banish often, we should also keep in mind we should practice often.

Step 6: Taking It All Back In

So you've done your magic, found what worked and what hasn't. You have your triumphs and your regrets. You, can, if you wish, set aside your tools when you don't need them. Let financial work be for when it is needed. Or perhaps you regularly read up on financial issues to keep fresh.

Or, now that you've done this work to understand finance magically, you can integrate financial ideas back into your magic. You have your magical systems - Sephiroth and elements, angels and gods. You have financial charts and systems, cycles, and terms.

The final stage of good financial magic is to map financial concepts back into your magical system. To fully make them part of what you do magically. Take the time to chart correspondences or attributes that you use. Much as magical correspondences deal with colors and animals and gems and so forth, you can integrate financial terms and concepts as well. Is currency Earth (possession) or Air (communication) to you? Is the act of investment mapped to the joyously outbursting Trigram of Lake or with the calculations of Wind? Financial discipline could be part of the austerity of Geburah or is it the intellectual activity of Hod?

Magic is, in the end, about the coherence of things, of correspondences, of microcosm and macrocosm. The end result of your financial magic can be making finance a complete part of your life and your magic. You come full circle from doing magical work on finance to integrating finance into your magical understanding. It makes your magic and yourself larger.

Vince Stevens is an IT Project Manager and experimental mage who lives on the west coast of the United States. He has engaged in both his technical and magical interests for over twenty years in an admittedly erratic, if enjoyable manner. His major focus is the use of magical and psychological practices to develop a completely integrated, magical life. For recreation he plays video games, works on websites, and speaks on various issues.

Money for Nothing: Making Wealth Magic Work
By Nick Farrell

While the rest of Christian civilisation was preaching the value of poverty, if you look at the old magical books you'll find that magicians were obsessed with wealth. Every second ritual was geared toward finding buried treasure or a gold mine. There are two deductions you can make from this. First, magicians were short of cash. Second they believed they had to dance through all sorts of ritual hoops to make themselves wealthy, rather than doing any real work for it. Of the lives of the magicians that we know about, it seems that most of their work was in vain; the majority of them died poor. Name any magician that did the job more or less full time and I will show you someone short of cash and living on the financial edge. If any magicians made a lot of cash from a good ritual then the technique is lost to us.

But if magic is supposed to give you everything you want, why is it that so much wealth magic goes belly up?

If you talk to anyone practising magic and ask them "if you are such great magician, why are you so broke?" if you do escape getting a broken nose, they will trot out one of a string of really good reasons. The most popular is that it's somehow immoral to use magic for material wealth. Another is that it some how distorts physical reality and the results will snap back and bite you. Others say that the path of magic to them is a spiritual thing and by concentrating on spirit you must reject the material.

These moral reasons are often strictly enforced by modern magicians. So much so that my former teacher David Goddard once did a day workshop on wealth magic based around a simple technique that would have taken ten minutes to explain. The rest of the workshop was spent explaining to people why they were allowed to do the magic to enable them to become wealthy. He said that the reason he did this was to overcome some of the intellectual and moral blocks people had about using magic for wealth.

However I'm not as nice. Anyone who has a passing knowledge of psychology will recognise a cop out when they see it and these moral reasons are some of the biggest. Whatever their moral leanings, most magicians try magic for wealth and have found that they couldn't get it to work. Instead of wondering why, they invent reasons that don't require them to look deeper into themselves. These reasons should be seen as the same lame "dog ate my homework" excuses that people give for keeping themselves from developing into better people.

It's a straight out fact that if magic works, then a practitioner should be able to create bucket loads of cash without too much trouble. All magical theory and history indicate it's possible. In fact it's considered easier than causing earthquakes, summoning armies, and changing someone into a fruit bat. If magic is a tool for using divine powers, why can't modern magicians use it to create a good environment for themselves? The answer really has to be found by looking at the magician and questioning about what sort of person is attracted to magic.

First you have to be honest. It does not matter what you *think* or *say* your motivations were for getting involved in magic, it's almost certainly really going to be about power. We want to be more powerful than our circumstances allow us to be. No, it isn't because you want to serve the light, it isn't because you want to help people or find the God within, or any other sanctimonious reason, it's because you are attracted to a path that promises power. But wait, power is a bad thing, I hear you cry. People like Lex Luther crave power and I want to be Superman or Wonder Woman. Yeah right. But Superman isn't famous for being powerless, in fact he only wins because he's more powerful than anyone else.

Over the years I have seen hundreds of applications to join the various esoteric groups I have been involved in and almost all of the initial motivations behind joining an occult group are power related. "I want knowledge", they tell you forgetting that knowledge is power. "I am looking for Wisdom" so you can do what? Be superior to someone who is "ignorant". "I seek the light of God", because normal people don't see God and you want to be 'special'.

There's nothing wrong with power. It's just that we have been programmed to shun it. We're taught that it's better to be a team player than to be the captain, or in the chorus than in centre stage. This is another cop out, the voices of the forces of darkness that want to keep you small. Those demons want to keep you from becoming and expressing your true individuality. The message of occultism is that you are a unique expression of God and that doesn't tally with a message from society that says we have to fit in and stay small.

Occultists, when they start this path, have usually worked this out in some measure. This is because they don't fit into society. They are what Colin Wilson called "Outsiders" who do not "fit in". Wilson said that one of the flaws of Outsiders is that they either over-emphasise the physical or are overly emotional. The people who overemphasize the physical become isolated because they are adrenaline junkies going to war or flinging themselves off skyscrapers. The people who overemphasize the emotional are softy romantics who sit in their bedrooms penning angst poetry about how unloved they are. Both give up on the real task of creating truthful meaning from life by being overly active or overly passive. While an Outsider lives at the edge and challenges cultural values. They create their own Inner Kingdoms and/or drift through life.

In other words, *outsiders suffer from a lack of power*. Some of this powerlessness is beaten into them by society and their families who want them to conform. Rather than fight their way into society they would rather sit back and moan about it in their various fantasy worlds; worlds that occultism makes all the more intense. They still crave power, but have to justify their lack of powerlessness to themselves. Therefore they invent cop outs. They make society "material" so that their "spirituality" doesn't have to mix with it. They seek to escape the rat race and thus allow such a system to continue unchecked. They talk about having spiritual cleansing, while at the same time are unable to find time to have a bath. This is not a new age hippy lifestyle I'm attacking; this state of affairs exists even among the more right-wing occult groups.

The path of an Outsider searching for God is a quest for power. But this shouldn't be a power which is over others, it should be a self-power. The new age movement calls this process empowerment and unfortunately there isn't a better word in the dictionary to describe it. Since we're talking about quests, I should mention that the Holy Grail, long castrated by those who would have turned it into a symbol of the Divine Feminine is missing the fact that it too is a symbol of power. Lancelot was powerless because of his neurotic love of Guinevere which was why he couldn't see it. His son who was an embodiment of power was able to take it.

So our average occultist, who is starting the path, believes in him or herself about as much as he or she believes in the ability of a rifle to stop a rogue bull elephant with a bull clip attached to its testicles. They have a huge task on their hands attracting wealth and power because their personalities aren't the natural place for such abilities to grow.

Magical Principles

Most magical work involves visualisation that is charged with emotion and will. Basically you see something happening as clearly as possible and will it to happen so that it feels that it already has happened. You can enhance this process by the use of symbols which are a bit like pre-made visualisations. The goal of this is to make your visualisations alive and as real as possible.

Most people do magic every second of the day. They are just not aware of the process which is why they aren't magicians. They get up and visualise what their day will be, good, bad, or indifferent. They charge these mental images, normally with their fears, and aren't surprised when they all manifest. Those who believe in themselves, or find life good, tend to be more optimistic and therefore, when shit happens, it is usually happening to someone else.

In my book *Magical Pathworking*, I describe how the universe is basically God's dream and everything is connected by symbols. Since we are part of God, we create our universe in the same way and our life is symbolic of who we are. I suggested various methods of playing around with those symbols so that we can not only see who we are but change ourselves and our environment. What I suggested is that we all carry in our psyches an Inner Kingdom which we rule according to our own perceptions. Some people make a pig's ear of it, others are masters of their Inner Kingdoms, while the majority or us do some things better than others. Therefore, before our occultist can progress he or she must become empowered at the level of his or her Inner Kingdom.

This is not an easy task to do. The average Inner Kingdom of an outsider is often messier than their bedrooms. Cluttered with failure they often find their Inner Kingdom is ruled by circumstance, bad habit, and laziness. Symbolically they are the prodigal prince who has left the Kingdom in the hands of the Grand Vizier who has done his best to take control and doesn't want the prince to take his rightful place on the throne. If you really were the King or Queen of your environment the Grand Vizier would be a dependable character -- he makes everything you believe in happen. However if he is in charge all he does is maintain the status quo. He uses the symbols that you believe in and creates an Inner Kingdom which is usually less than desirable. For example you might have had a bad boss who fired you for no reason. That boss becomes a symbol for every employer in a position of power over you. Your Grand Vizier will dust off that symbol every time you encounter an employer and make sure that you will encounter similar situations.

In the case of our new occultist, there will be few symbols of wealth or power. However, there will be a lot of symbols of a lack of these things. They perform a ritual to make themselves wealthy and this plants a seed within their Inner Kingdom that this is how things should be. However it's a classic case of a seed falling on stony ground or among weeds. There is just so much in the Inner Kingdom that will strangle such rituals that they are pointless.

Ritual does have some safe-guards to override these problems. By calling on powerful forces in the universe, such as Angels and Gods, it's possible to override our feelings of being small. Fully charged by a good working, and the god-form speaking through us, it's possible to really feel that this time there will be change. We can push ourselves over our barriers and believe it's possible to be wealthy or powerful. However, our own negativity about becoming wealthy will eventually shine through and ultimately any ritual will fail, or worse we will lose anything we gain. One of the most common requests magicians get is for lottery numbers, yet this sudden wealth is totally incompatible with those who cannot hold such symbols within their Inner Kingdom.

This can be seen in the case of the non-magician Viv Nicholson who was one of the UK's pools winners. In 1961, Viv and Keith Nicholson were living on a £7-a-week trainee miner's wage bringing up three kids in a tiny terraced home in Castleford, Yorkshire. Then they won the equivalent of £3 million on the football pools. Far from making them happy they spent the money too quickly. Keith died behind the wheel of his expensive car, Viv ended up with a string of husbands who married her for the money that she had already spent. She became bankrupt and later became a devout Jehovah's Witness. Wealth was not part of her Inner Kingdom and was rejected as fast as it entered.

You need to be extremely self-confident and sure of your own views on money and power to do a successful ritual to win something like the lottery. When I was working on a local newspaper and covering the first lottery winners, I was surprised how few really poor people were winners. Most of the people who won the lottery were already comfortable and they would be spending the money fairly prudently. When a poor person was a winner, you found they had to give away a lot of their winnings to friends and family and didn't keep much of it. These were the same behaviour patterns they had for most of their lives. When money came in, they spent it. When a huge amount of money came in they just spent more of it.

Using magic to inject more money into the lives of such people is not really going to change them much. It will not work for you either.

Methods of Getting Rid of the Inner Blocks

By knowing why and how wealth magic works through my psyche I can work with it rather than futilely do rituals which aren't going to get me far.

In *Magical Pathworking* I described a method of getting into your Inner Kingdom using the magic mirror of pathworking. After getting into an altered state you visualise a Celtic or medieval village that you're supposed to rule.

In your mind's eye you wander around the village and try and get as many details as possible. You then interpret these random symbols as if you would a dream. At the center of your village is the Hall of the Hero, which represents your inner state. In my version, it's based on the Cabalistic Tree of Life design. It is a throne room from which a person is supposed to rule his/her warriors (areas of personal activity) and outer world. Some find that their Hall is empty, or that they were lacking some key elements. Some very stressed and busy people find that their warriors made too much noise and have to be silenced.

As you face the throne there are doors to two rooms behind you and two rooms in front of you. Since this is based on Cabbalah the door behind you on the right hand side is the room which is to do with love and partnerships. The one behind you is the library and it is the place of intellectual pursuits. The door on your left hand is that of the armoury and shows you the state of your energy and ability to do things. The one on your left hand is the most interesting because this is the room of the treasury. If you go in there, you will see symbols relating to the state of your power and wealth. A number of people find that this room is empty; one person found a huge pile of money which has never been used and had cobwebs growing all around it.

While this information does give you powerful clues as to the state of your Inner Kingdom, it's always better to resolve these issues before leaving. If you have no cash, go back to the throne room and order your soldiers to collect the taxes that are owed. One of the warriors might tell you that someone has been thieving the cash and thus taking your power. It's worthwhile trying to find out who and

50

under what circumstance. During my experiments with this system I found the missing money in the room relating to my partnership, which at the time was neurotic and twisted.

Jumping Hurdles

While I believe that fixing your Inner Kingdom is the key to breaking down the blocks to allowing material magic to happen, there are a few practical tips that might help too.

One way of overcoming the psychological defences we have against money and wealth is to work magic that will provide us with what we want. In other words, rather than do a ritual for $30,000 to get us a really good car, we do a ritual to get the car instead. We visualise ourselves driving the car and surround ourselves with the energy from an appropriate ritual to make it happen. The downside of this is that we often have to really want that car. I find that a ritual like that opens doors for me to obtain what I want only if I really want it. I find that I get commissioned to do lots more extra work and have to work harder. This is because in my Inner Kingdom there is a belief that I will not get what I want if I don't do some work. It is probably some work ethic thing from my Protestant past. However for some strange reason I have never lost money when betting on horses, probably because I don't do it that often.

Other ways of getting around our blocks on money is to try lots of rituals for smaller amounts. When I am experimenting with different types of techniques, I find that $10 is a good value that will not get stopped by my psyche. When working with entities sometimes it is a good symbol of a transfer of power from them to me if they agree to allow me to get a five pound note in mysterious circumstances. This ranges from finding them on the street, to accidentally short changing a taxi driver (which is such a miracle as to be impossible). Obviously, you are not going to become wealthy in five dollar bursts, but if you can get this to work, then you might find that $10 is easier and later $100. That is assuming that you aren't killed for short changing a taxi driver of $100.

One thing might strike you as odd about all this. Material magic is often called Low Magic because it has a result on the lower plains of manifestation. Higher Magic, which targets the higher spirituality realms, includes alchemy on the personality and the soul. I am suggesting that for a person to perform Low Magic successfully they have to have had some experience with Higher Magical techniques first.

In fact, I would go as far as saying that the divisions between low and high magic are so arbitrary it's misleading and better not to make a distinction at all. The idea that spirit is somehow higher is one of the reasons why people wanting to use magic to achieve material success fail. If you see the universe as a manifestation of One Being, then what it does in matter is as equally spiritual as what it does in the higher planes. If you accept the Emerald Tablet, what is happening on the material planes is a direct result of what goes on in the heavens and visa versa. Both "high" and "low" magic need each other.

Another important block can be removed by simply shutting up about the magic you work. A lot of magical groups and training systems swear their magicians to secrecy. Some do so because they believe that somewhere in the group's mythology there was a Witchfinder General with a packet of matches. But there is a more practical reason for it. You build your magic out of thought and charged emotion. You want your image sitting on the astral like a big magnet bringing what you want to you. If you're dumb enough to tell someone about this thought form they will have views about it. Most likely they will be neutral, but all it takes is someone to think "that sounds slightly nuts to me" and your lovingly created thought-form will take a battering. As we have said, it's hard enough to get material magic past the blocks in your own psyche without bringing in other people's problems.

It's best to do the ritual and not think about it again until the results start coming in. Modern occultists shoot their mouths off far too often. The older members of the Golden Dawn group with whom I was lucky to work with were almost pathologically secretive. As a local journalist, I wrote the obituary of one of them not knowing that he was even a member of the group and he turned out to be one of the chiefs. However, their magic really was something to watch. It was just you couldn't talk about it either.

Material Magic Needs Concrete Answers

Earlier I mentioned how whenever I did wealth magic I found that I had to do a lot more work. This is one aspect that many would-be occultists forget when they are working material magic. It isn't enough to create the right symbol on the astral plane to draw the cash to you, you have to do some donkey work on the ground too. There are philosophical and practical reasons for this. When you perform magic you are working on the astral plane, the one above this level of reality. The skill in making it work is to allow it to transfer itself from that plane to the material. Otherwise it will simply stay there. A material ritual which is stuck on the astral plane will partly work, it will just draw lots of power, dreams of wealth, opportunity and perhaps ideas for making cash. However, any actual money showing up will be dependant on the magician performing an actual act on the material levels. Simplistically you have to buy a lottery ticket after doing a ritual to win the lottery. It all seems like stating the obvious, but you'll be amazed how many people do material magic and then sit around and wait for a bunch of elves to show up with a trunk on their front door step.

For example, a ritual might not generate money, but a good idea about how to raise money. It might a blinding flash, but if it checks out, you would be wise to do something to make it happen. A ritual might generate a better job which might make you more cash, but you have to take the new role to benefit from it. Generally if you have a ritually generated opportunity it will come with a feeling of absolute certainty. There will be lots of assistances from other people who have had similar ideas, perhaps influenced unconsciously by your ritual. Either way you are going to have to do something.

The adept of material magic is a practical person who sees earthly opportunities before he or she thinks of the astral ones. There was a recent case of a person who asked me to make a talisman to improve the sales for his company. His sales manager was getting through to clients, but couldn't close deals and the CEO thought a talisman would make customers more forthcoming. Really the problem was that the sales manager, who was a good manager of a technical support team, was a lousy salesperson. The answer wasn't a talisman, but to take the sales manager away from a job that wasn't expressing who he really was.

If someone is hurting your career by being a bully, you can set a demon onto them, but it's much more effective to evoke the Human Resources manager. Sure, a good rite to remove the bully from your life is a good idea, but again the mechanics of the desired change will always come though your own action.

Technique

One of the problems with performing rituals or visualisation techniques to generate wealth or abundance is that there is a lack of common symbols – what makes my buns dance may not mean abundance to you. Golden coins, which have been a symbol of wealth for centuries, are still powerful, but have been dramatically weakened by the idea of paper money. So if you are going to do magic involving cash you should use or visualise dollar bills and pound notes.

Since material magic is closer to your reality, you should look for symbols that mean wealth to you and use them. Playing around with these symbols in a fun and interesting way is the key to success. Below are a few of my ideas, but you should try to work out some of your own.

You have heard the phrase "money doesn't grow on trees" but wealth magic has been associated with plants for centuries. One of my favourite traditions comes from Bulgaria and is probably from Ancient Thrace. It involves taking two colours of thread, one red and one white, and weaving them together to make a martinitza. On the first day of March you tie this thread around a friend's wrist.

People wear the thread for a month, or until they see a stork, and then hang it onto a tree which is just budding and it is supposed to bring wealth and good fortune. Magically what they are doing is linking their energy, which is imprinted into the red and white thread after being worn for a month, and linking it to the growing power of the tree.

Obviously this rite is connected to spring and can only be done in March, but it is possible to work out some ideas based around this. I made a traditional rite more powerful by making a big ritual of tying the martinitza around a tree which was associated with my star sign. As I tied it I would say:

"As I bind this symbol of myself to this tree, so shall I draw its energy upon me and use it for wealth and health."

A few years ago I experimented fairly successfully with a fun idea involving taking a pound coin[6] and a pot of earth. Ritual space is prepared with the pot and the coin on an altar in the middle. There should also be some 'holy' water which is made with what ever ritual you would normally use and some incense.

Consecrate the coin by rubbing some of the water on it saying:
"Creature of Earth, you who are a symbol of my material wealth, I cleanse you for my use."
Then pass the coin through the incense smoke and say:
"Creature of Earth, you who are a symbol of my material wealth, I cleanse you for my use."

---

[6] A dollar bill will also work.

Go to the east with the coin and say:

"Creature of Earth, you who are a symbol of my material wealth, I empower you with the name _____ [7] May you become inflamed with his /her power, so that you will be come a seeds that shall grow into a tall tree. May you become this as I chant (his/her) holy name."

Circumambulate around the altar clockwise chanting the Divine Name. You should do this until in your mind's eye, the coin starts to glow golden. Place the coin on the altar and pick up the pot.

Drop some of the water in the earth saying:

"Creature of Earth, you who are a symbol of my material world, I cleanse you for my use."

Then pass the pot through the incense smoke and say:

"Creature of Earth, you who are a symbol of my material world, I cleanse you for my use."

Take the coin and say:

"Thus do I plant this divine wealth into my material world."

Plant the coin. Take the water and sprinkle some on the soil and say:

"Drop you dew from heaven. Nourish this plant forever more."

Take a bit of ash and sprinkle it on the plant and say:

"From the powers of the Divine Fire my wealth grows."

Once you have done this rite, you have a choice on how you continue it. I ritually watered it with holy water once a week and visualised the tree growing. Over a period of about a year I visualised the tree getting taller, until I had to shift it to the garden where I repotted it. Unfortunately, I moved house so it never got it taller than me, but my business did quite well after that.

Nick Farrell was born as the sun rose on August 4 1965. This made him a Leo with Leo ascendant which has been a curse for humanity ever since. His family exported themselves to New Zealand where he grew up in a place called Paekakariki, which few people can spell. At the age of ten he was suckered into becoming a Baptist after a very clever minister convinced him he was responsible for the death of a bloke 2000 years ago. After he realised he had been conned, he went out in search of God, who for argument's sake he called Jeff (because it would be silly to have a supreme being called Nigel). His path led him into the Builders of the Adytum and from there into Servants of the Light, the Pharos, and finally into the Golden Dawn. For the last

---

[7] You should use a Divine Name of a God or Goddess that you associate with material well being here. I used the cabbalistic name Adonai Malek.

ten years he has been working exclusively in that system, although he still has not talked directly to Jeff who appears to be on answer phone. He has written several books on occult subjects including Making Talismans, Magical Pathworking, Egyptian Shamanism, Gathering the Magic, and the Druidic Order of Pendragon.

He works for a living writing tabloid IT stories for www.theinquirer.net and lectures in Journalism at the American University. He lives at the foot of a mountain in Sofia, Bulgaria and is married to Didi. He just finishing writing a Sci-Fi novel which includes Jeff called "When a Tree Falls".

Creating an Abundance of Wealth
by Sage NightStar

My personal Wiccan philosophy that I've stuck to for 15 years is that the Universe is abundant and full possibilities. My friend, Samantha, (that name just oozes Magick doesn't it?), has trouble with this theory because she believes that the word "abundant" can manifest both positive and negative circumstances if we are not specific about what it is we want an abundance of. But, as a Witch I can assure you that I use that word with the most positive of intentions and it has paid off for me time and time again.

Ethical and positive intent is not the only deliberate thinking principle that affects the outcome of magick. The other mindset that impacts magickal success more so than intent is belief not only in the magick, but also in your personal conviction as a Witch, Mage, Magician, Conjurer, Craft Practitioner, etc. Magick is created when your purpose and faith are used to manifest and direct energy on the spiritual level. As you become directly engaged in the magick after the spell is cast, the energy builds and increases the probability that your goal will be realized. I call this DOING THE WORK!

Case in point, if you need a better paying job, you perform your chosen spell or magickal formula and then follow it up with proactive participation such as doing a thorough job search including sending out resumes, scheduling interviews, establishing references, etc. By doing so, your chances of landing that job are increased considerably vs. sitting by the cell phone waiting for the perfect job offer. Selfishness and too many conditions may keep us from doing the work on the mundane level to achieve financial success. There is NO perfect job, even if you run your own business. There is always a boss, either someone above you in the company, or the customer. Despite the infinite number of infomercials that run all hours of the night, there is NO GET RICH QUICK SCHEME that delivers on promises of a high income with little effort and little time. And, I couldn't let this one go without saying it, "MONEY DOES NOT GROW ON TREES!". Is it always necessary to do the work on the mundane level to reinforce magickal success? Not always. But, I guarantee that it will make a difference when you are conjuring to increase personal or professional wealth.

Do you have enough money, or is there too much month at the end of the money? In other words, do you experience a shortage of monthly cash flow and find yourself wishing there were more, while fantasizing about what you would do if you won the lottery tomorrow or inherited millions from a distance relative that you had never heard of or met. Ask yourself this: how much money do you blow on what you consider must haves and what is in reality addictions, such as alcohol and smokes? How much do you spend at the local Starbucks each week, paying as much as a 400-500% mark up on a gourmet cup of coffee? How often do you let the credit card companies get the best of your good judgment, building an incredible amount of debt and taking half your life and even more than half your income to pay back what you owe at an interest rate that should be outlawed? We live in a world where we literally throw money away towards items that we really do not need to survive, and we waste time watching TV, web surfing, talking on the cell phone, emailing and text messaging, or doing other "busy" work instead of pursuing a desired goal that brings us success. But wealth is not just about money, and you must decide what wealth means to you and how you are going to create it. Wealth is about resources and balance such as spending your time wisely and taking care of your mind, body and spirit in order to perform the work on both the magickal and mundane levels.

Is it necessary to earn an income of 6 figures or more to achieve the quality of life that you desire? Absolutely not! Many people earn a modest salary, budget what they have and not what they don't have, live simply, look for ways not to spend, shop thriftily, use money-saving resources and strategies, and end up with more money in the bank than most people dream of. And when an emergency rises or there is something extra special within their reach, they have the resources for what they need and want. Some of the wealthiest people I know are also the thriftiest. There's one friend of mine that is just down right cheap, and he has more money than the Gods put together.

Money is a form of energy, and it is an energy that you have complete control over after taxes are taken. How you earn or receive money and how you spend it will ultimately affect the results of any magickal undertaking. For instance, if you acquire money dishonestly, spend it on something frivolous and then spell cast for additional money to pay the necessary bills, the chances of the magick manifesting in your favor are considerably reduced. This is a simple act of karma and misuse of your magickal abilities. You must also be conscientious about asking for more of your fair share and remember the needs of others.

The challenge to having more money is that it gives you more life choices, which on the surface makes you believe that your life will be less stressful. But, with so many choices the decision/selection process can add more pressure than having only limited choices. For example, I have at least sixty pairs of shoes and can never make up my mind which pair to wear. Having less of a shoe selection would sure make getting dressed in the morning a more relaxing experience. I could buy fewer pairs of shoes and put that money towards something I really need or save it for a large expense or unforeseen circumstance. Focusing on what we need rather than what we want can also influence our financial status. Who needs sixty pairs of shoes?

Having a spiritual and magickal plan accompanied by a mundane success plan will help you to manifest immediate and long term financial abundance and security, providing you with what you need, a little extra, and even resources that will allow you to give back offerings of thanks to the Goddess/God and to society as a way to keep things in balance.

Assuming that you know the basics to spell casting and magick 101, I won't bore you with color, crystal, and herb correspondences or astrological influences for wealth, abundance, prosperity, financial growth, etc. but I will share both Witchcraft and ordinary strategies, techniques and studies that have resulted in the creation of abundance for myself and others that I have developed my entire Wiccan practice and belief around.

People who have achieved financial wealth, abundance and prosperity have an undeniable love and passion for their chosen career and work, and they are possessed by success. I call this state "moonstruck". They may have a vision that others think is completely insane or impossible, but eventually their vision becomes reality. Their business strategies may be considered deluded but ultimately work. They put in long hours remaining focused on the outcome and not on the busy work. They do not take no for an answer. And, they never, ever, ever, give up. Practicing a moonstruck work ethic will produce results. However, it does require focus, commitment, patience and sacrifice, so it is important to surround yourself with those who understand your goals and can provide you with the support that will feed your passion and not distract you from it. There have been times in my life where I have been moonstruck with my profession and spiritual work and have complimented this practice with spells to achieve specific objectives and outcomes. I've also made nontraditional lifestyle choices that support my goals. For example, I chose not to have children and married a man who is neither jealous nor possessive, respects my work, and gives me the independence and freedom to do what I need to do without questioning my commitment to him.

The spells I've worked to support my professional career goals include using a technique to build and increase magical energy by deepening the level of my focus, what I refer to as mindful magick. I do not build energy by drumming, chanting, dancing, etc. I consider raising energy in this manner to be superficial (That being said, I've had some discussions with others about the idea of combining spiritual magick with stage magic as a technique to build energy—a topic for another article!). Instead, I build the energy as I do the work on the mundane level all along keeping my mind focused on the outcome I desire. For example, if I'm writing a grant to fund a special project, as I develop each component of the grant on the mundane level, my mind is raising energy on the spiritual level that will be released in ritual when the grant is completed and ready for submission.

When it comes to increasing my personal cash flow, my biggest successes is using magick that involves in some way actual money. For example, I've created a financial abundance box that I use to store all the monthly bills in. The box is green, of course, and decorated with actual German cash (I chose German currency because I'm creating my own tradition of Witchcraft based on German history and the Brockenberg Mountain where the Goddess Freya reins.) in addition to other Wiccan symbols, jewels, crystals, and symbols of deities associated with prosperity, abundance, etc. One look at that box and you just know it is magickal and serves a special purpose—it ensures that there is always money for the bills and some to save for a rainy day. I've also created wishing wells and abundance cauldrons simply by creating and charging these items to grow coins from my wallet on a daily basis and even small currency bills and before I know it, I have several hundred dollars ready to pay off a bill, invest or treat myself to something special. These techniques simply apply the like-attracts-like law.

Another more sophisticated approach I've utilized to create prosperity is what I call magickal model channeling. It is a skill that requires a wonderful imagination and the ability to personify another individual without losing your sense of self in the process. It is a technique of selecting and channeling the success of someone whose professional work, efforts, etc. I admire such as J. K. Rowling (need I say more). I do this by researching information about their lives and collecting tangible items associated with them, such as books/publications they may have authored, photographs of them in their work/effort, and using these items to create an altar for meditating on their successes, and I then channel their successes as I perform both the mundane and magickal work towards a specific goal. I've performed well in my profession due to magick model channeling, and I now have a career and opportunities in the magickal community that I had only fantasized about.

Some additional suggestions follow for you to consider as you create your own magick towards wealth, prosperity and abundance:

Fridays are the best days for business success such as increasing sales or closing a deal. Perform spells not only to increase financial gain but to decrease unnecessary spending. Perform Tarot readings, scrying, or other divination techniques as a part of developing your spiritual and mundane plans. Never lend money to anyone. Use the color orange in business success spells. Create and decorate wealth altars using the colors of green, gold and silver. Pay bills on time. Use coupons and rebate offers. Perform magick working with Queen Juno, the highest Roman Goddess who protected the finances of the Roman Empire. Do not practice wealth, prosperity or abundance magick when Mercury is in retrograde. Use bay leaves in money magick. Banish negativity from your life by using graveyard dirt, cayenne pepper, black pepper, nettle, dragon's blood, and sage. Fold currency in your wallet with the face side pointing toward you and not away from you. Save! To keep abundance flowing, work your magick each month during the full moon.

Beware that there will be tough times. For some reason the magick doesn't manifest because the Goddess has a better plan for us, or just when we've saved a significant amount some major expense comes up such as a home or car repair we weren't expecting, or we get laid off from work without notice. It happens to the best of us Witches. But, remember that a lack of wealth, prosperity and abundance builds character and in the end we can't take it with us, but we can move on to the next life knowing that we are a bit closer to being Goddess/God like.

Living the magickal life,

Sage NightStar

Sage NightStar is an eclectic Wiccan High Priestess, a member of the Sisters of the Burning Branch, and currently creating her own tradition of German Witchcraft to be known as the Brockenberg Path. She is the author of *Witcheries*, a regular column in "Priestess Pathways" published by the Sisters of the Burning Branch, and she is currently working on her first book project, "After the Spell is Cast". Sage is a professional special event director and non-profit manager and fund raiser. She is experienced in media relations and is a published journalist and special correspondent. Sage is also the creator and proprietor of "Goddess Goods by Sage", her own line of aromatherapy products. She is a Capricorn, partnered with a much younger man (which she highly recommends), and believes that we can have more than one soul mate and love many during our lifetime. Sage is the guardian to a devoted Lhasa Apso named Ori and her familiar and snobby cat, Bastet. For more information about Sage, please visit her at www.sagenightstar.com.

Cattle Magic: Embracing a Paradigm of Wealth
By Kiya Nicoll

Magical work begins in the mind; it is shaped by the assumptions found there about the way the world works. Axioms slant the shape of results, the way the will can apply its leverage, the ways that energies can flow. A magician begins with the belief that the will can affect the world; beliefs about reality and the way the will can be brought to bear are a part of paradigm, and thus a part of how that force manifests. I expect most any will-worker will have a few experiences with spells that failed or unraveled because someone – often the magician themselves – did not believe in some part of the process or the results. Paradigms of wealth and its acquisition can enhance or sabotage the best efforts of the magician, often in very subtle ways. I frame wealth work as cattle magic; to explain cattle magic, I start with writing.

One of the frequent pieces of advice that gets given to budding novelists is "Write what you know."

Like most pieces of writing advice, this has the potential to create huge swaths of insecurity out of nowhere, as the would-be writer starts to wonder what counts as knowing. "I've worked a desk job all my adult life; can I write about living as a nomadic horseman? Can I write about spaceships exploring Alpha Centauri? Can I write about Wales? I've never been to Wales." All the worlds of wonder that are lacking come up, dominating the thoughts, and turning the entire question on its head. What began as a focus on resources immediately becomes a focus on lacks.

That same writer may have a quirky, but insightful way of looking at the personalities they have met in that twenty years of working customer service; may have had experiences in childhood outside the kenning of the people in the cubes next door; may have a brilliant turn of phrase just waiting for the opportunity to set pen to paper. And often, discouraged, they will say, "I have nothing to offer, I have no story in me", because the story they want to tell has some piece that cannot be assembled from their intimate personal experience of the world.

There is a blindness there, an inability to count the cows one has. The model of scarcity is a potent and demanding one, full of inadequacy and the inability to escape one's lot. It has its roots in a variety of places, threaded through pieces of surrounding culture:

"blessed are the poor", "keeping up with the Joneses", "You load sixteen tons, and what do you get? Another day older and deeper in debt."

The culture I grew up in had very little allowance for counting the cattle I had. Not only is it steeped in the false scarcity of advertising, but in the deeply-ground insecurities: is my body good enough, attractive enough, toned enough, and strong enough? Is my job experience good enough, broad enough, advanced enough, going to qualify me for this new position or that raise? Am I lovable? Am I acceptable? Am I adequate? What am I missing, and what do I need to get to patch that hole?

This is a paradigm that sabotages wealth. Not only does it approach the question from an attitude of lacking, and thus tends to perpetuate that emptiness, but everything that is gained will serve only to mend a gap, bring the ledger a little bit out of the red, a little closer to zero. There is no real potential for positive gain here, only, perhaps, getting less and less deficient.

I talk about cattle, in this, for a reason: the use of cattle to represent both wealth and the power to gain and sustain wealth spans many cultures. It is a primeval symbol, at least for cultures in much of the Eastern Hemisphere; even a will-worker who does not prefer to use the symbologies of the many cultures which have considered cattle to be symbols of riches and fertility (the root of ancient wealth) will still be familiar with the astrological sign of Taurus the Bull, the sign of prosperity, wealth, material goods, and satisfaction (Part of my own interest in cattle magic derives from the fact that I have Chiron in Taurus in my natal chart, and thus wrestle constantly with the questions of wealth and lack.).

To work within this paradigm of cattle magic, it is important to begin with wealth. Many of those aforementioned ancient cultures kept this in mind; the first letter of our own alphabet derives, if one chases it back far enough, from a Phoenician character shaped like an ox-head. Runeworkers will already be familiar with the fact that the rune for wealth and cattle, fehu, is the F in the futhark. Whether it is the Hindu declaration of the cow as the mother of the gods, the Egyptian fertility principle embodied in the Apis bull and the sky-cow who rebirths and rejuvenates the sun, or the Norse primeval cow Audumla, who nourished the first frost giant and freed the first god from the ice, cattle are deep in mythologies as a source of life, strength, and riches, from the very beginning.

So, what does it mean to start with wealth? This goes beyond merely "What are my material assets" (and the frequent question,

64

"What am I missing?"); it includes assessing and recognizing skills, aptitudes, the material and emotional support of partners, friends, and family. It includes potential. It includes awareness of opportunity. The farmer with three cows doesn't get to have a herd of fifty by saying, "But I only have three cows"; he gets there by saying, "I have three cows, and my neighbor has a bull."

Wealth brings forth further wealth in many different forms. In addition to being symbols of currency, cattle have also been symbols of fecundity and virility. They embody a generative principle; one cow can become more, the labor and milk from the cow produce other forms of wealth (it was arguably the value of their milk, dung, and labor that led to the forbidding of the slaughter of cattle in India). To a traditional Zulu, cattle mean not only the opportunity to meet a partner (as the boys will take them for water at the same place the girls collect water for the household) but the ability to offer an appropriate gift to a girl's parents so that they will be accepted as a potential marriage partner: cattle wealth translates directly into family life, not merely the support for a family but the root of a family itself. The ability to acquire new skills, acquire new knowledge, acquire new contacts, broaden and deepen one's capacities, is a form of wealth inseparable from that principle of fertility. The writer who stalled out on "Write what you know" has the capacity to imagine and extrapolate, the capacity to learn about nomadic horsemen or the weather over Swansea; not knowing these things now does not mean that they cannot be known.

Developing wealth requires a sense of scale. The farmer is not going to go from three cows to fifty in a single breeding season. Patience is essential, and the recognition that even if one is building towards a particular level of wealth, that does not mean that the steps taken towards it will work immediately and provide instant gratification. The "Sure, when I win the lottery" attitude does not take a step forward; it is rooted in that same sense of scarcity that locks directed work towards gain into a pattern of obsession with what is not there.

An example: when I was a small child, I was painfully aware of my inadequacies in strength, and became convinced that there was no way that I would ever be able to develop muscle. This persisted for many years, until someone suggested to me that I try lifting soup cans. Taking that small first step, smaller than any I had imagined before, made it possible for me to take larger steps; the piece I needed was the sense of scale, of what I could do to work with what I had. So long as my strength was inadequate to do any of the things that were presented to me as strength-building exercises, I was soaked in the fact of my lack of ability. I actually had everything that I needed to begin except the understanding of how to apply it, the ability to take the first small step.

The first small steps are a part of managing the cattle: talking to the neighbor with the bull, perhaps, to extend that metaphor. Building the herd is more complicated than the first steps, however; those cattle require care. Simply having a cow – a skill, a resource, a piece of knowledge – does nothing unless that is applied in an area where that skill is useful. Further, simply taking a job on the basis of those things will not necessarily lead to a sense of wealth; skills can be overworked, aptitudes drained, so while this may lead to financial gain, the emotional costs put one deeper in the hole.

Those cattle are potentially the source of many kinds of wealth. One can simply accumulate – breed and buy and raid up to that fifty-cow herd, if that is what one wants. Or one can nurture particular traits – breed for the best milk cow, use the labor behind the plow, accumulate enough cattle to supply the needs of one's family and stop there because going beyond that is labor for no significant gain, or hitch those oxen up to a cart to move material goods from here to there. All of these require a sense rooted in wealth, a knowledge of what would be sufficiency: the knowing what feeds the actual need, what counts as being rich.

What one wants to be able to do is inseparable from genuine wealth. Building the herd meaningfully takes knowing what to develop, what to select for, which cows to sell and trade away because they do not produce enough gain of the sort desired. Wealth can be conceptualized as one form of the power to accomplish one's goals in the world; without goals, one's material capacity can remain aimless and undefined, and the questions "Is this enough? Do I need more?" cannot be answered. Scarcity slides in here, around the edges, the same lack of knowledge that stymies that writer faced with "Write what you know." Priorities and values shape what is wealth; a jet-setting life of high prestige and tremendous monetary gain may not satisfy the wealth-sense of someone who wants a quiet, sedate, and comfortable life. Each person might well consider the other poor in terms of what they value most, but they are simply breeding different cattle.

For a more esoteric bent, cattle have long been linked with sacrifices and offerings to the gods. From the Golden Calf created as an offering by the lapsed Hebrew tribes, through to the bull's blood baptism of the Mithraists, to the major public rituals of the Greeks in which the thighbones were burned for the gods and the meat distributed to the people, even to the modern-day miracle reported in which icons of Ganesha took milk offerings, the gifts of cattle and their products have long been a part of spiritual work. Here, the wealth is translated in form: the material abundance represented by the offered cattle being translated into a petition for further fertility, offered as a gift, translated to some form of immortality, or given as a proof of willingness to put forth labor in both the material and magical realms. A magician working with cattle magic must consider what need be sacrificed to work that magic: what effort must be put out, what material goods must be dedicated, what time must be pledged. The translation of wealth from one form to the other does not happen without expenditure.

Many cultures that have been extensive herders have also been adept at the cattle raid. The material wealth gained there might be only transitory, but it was still significant: the genuine gain was primarily a matter of prestige, the accomplishment of doing something, a proof of ability. Working cattle magic includes taking risks, striving for something that will produce recognition and work within systems of status. This is the magic of the person who makes a stock market gamble, builds a startup company from the ground up, or quits that stable, responsible job in order to find something to do that they really love. It rests in recognition of opportunity and application of skill, and balances out the steady gains of patient breeding and trading with the possibility of dramatic gain, or at least dramatic change of circumstance.

Cattle magic also requires breaking the links between resources and moral correctness. If the prospect of seeking employment with the skills one loves to use gets called "selling out", then opportunities are lost to feed those cows. The cows don't care about whether or not it's a perversion of art to be paid for that work, or whether someone could really make more of themselves than the job that leaves them enough time and energy to write that book about nomadic horsemen in the evenings after dinner, or whether it's more responsible to keep the steady job than try the startup with the great new idea. The cows just want to be fed. A teacher I studied with for a while was fond of telling the story of how she used to do wealth magic all the time, but had a deep-seated belief that money was somehow corrupting or dirty. Obviously, she would say, that meant her spells didn't work. If someone's life isn't built in a way that allows it to sustain the resources they have, their wealth of energy, ideas, skills, and competences, their social networks and their family, then their cattle will start to starve, and things fall into a state of genuine scarcity.

In a state of genuine scarcity, wealth is difficult; even the concept is hard to reach. Playing with paradigm alone will not stretch that paycheck enough to cover the rent and the groceries, no matter how much one wants it to. However, it may create space for options, presuming that need has not yet skinned the cattle. Need can devour even the possibilities of seeing opportunity if it comes to define the paradigm; without opportunity, without the option to change, stretch, or adjust, scarcity will kill each cow, one at a time, or even wholesale. It will devour options and flexibility and keep one locked into a hamster-wheel of finance, unable to get anywhere or see a way of acting that can get one somewhere better. Instead of the view looking towards expansion that cattle magic encourages, one can get trapped in the narrowing and inescapable treadmill of scarcity.

Moving Mindset Into Reality

So enough presentation of paradigm; time for a few examples of putting it into practice.

Working within an approach like what I call cattle magic does not always lend itself directly to specific workings of magic. It is, instead, a set of assumptions that underlie the work one does, wherever one draws the line between the pragmatic and the esoteric.

My first major lesson in cattle magic was not spellcraft; it came when I had just acquired a statue that was associated with my religious witchcraft practice. I wanted to display it properly and respectfully, and my first thought was, "I really don't have what I need for a proper altar space for it." After having a moment of scowling sadness at that point, I tried the approach, "Well, let me see what I do have." I had a flat surface and a green drape, so that was a start. "I could set up my feather fan behind her as a backdrop," I thought, then, and did so. I added some of my tools to the space, found a bowl to put in front of the statue for offerings, came across a votive candle holder, and finally found myself holding a little green man face that my father had given me, staring at the perfectly centered nail right over this impromptu altar. In fact, it turned out that I had everything I needed, including that highly coincidental and unplanned nail. Opening to the possibility of wealth completely satisfied my need for riches.

The second lesson was a matter of craft, of working with the making of tools. I was having a moment of flailing incoherence at the notion of crafting a wand; I had particular strictures I had to follow for that purpose. I mentioned this to a community of friends, and one of them said, "Oh, I have a tree of that particular wood that needs to be pruned. I'll send you some of the branches." A few weeks later, a mailing tube appeared with a good half-dozen potential wands, of various shapes and thicknesses, all because I opened up to the world and said, "This is part of what I need for this". The wealth of friendship brought it to me; it has brought most of the rest of the components for that piece together. The entire thing, a piece dedicated to the cow-headed goddess Hathor, whose domains include wealth, beauty, and abundance, is a work of the wealth of community: the wood from a friend, the feathers a gift from a lover, the stone, for the handle, a piece from a ritual done by my working magical group, a piece of gold bought from a friend who needed to be ransomed from the symbol of a dead marriage. Opening to the symbolism of the wealth of community has made finding the resources easy, and the results rich with meaning and the memories of all these ties.

The third lesson, the one that reaches a level of spellwork: a partner and I were working on something that rides that edge between the material and the magical: he wanted to build a collection of images to flesh out his library with missing pieces. The things put together in that structure were all small charms, in their way, recognized as having the potential to represent meaning, to manifest something. He and I have had discussions about resources and resource manipulation in the past, about scarcity and the power to affect the world with the applications of one's wealth; we talked about being able to see and recognize what one has.

He had gathered a collection of items to use for these images, mostly things collected from his various altars, and I had made a few suggestions for things to be done with them. While he was working with some of the pieces that were laid out on the table, I wandered a little, exploring his library and stopping next to his ritual altar, which had had its drawers partially emptied onto its surface as part of this project.

One of the items that had not been brought over to the working space was a small statuette of a long-horned cow. It was a greenish turquoise in color, lying down with its head turned to gaze to the side; overall, the impression was one of bucolic affability. I studied it for a moment, and then started to rummage through the bowl of his rune set, which he had carved into the faces of a collection of dollar coins.

I found the rune I was looking for just as he left the room for a bit, and thus had the opportunity to put the pieces together: the statue set out, with the *fehu* rune carved into a coin tucked against the cow's side, with her head apparently turned to study it with one eye.

69

Here was an image he needed, something to fill out the scope of awareness and expression, something to serve as a charm and an awareness: you have these things, this cattle magic, this was something I could gather for you and present. Remember this.

He came back and spotted the tableau as I had established it, and stopped, and there was the moment of lighting up with recognition, recognizing exactly what was in that spell. It was made of what he already had, this opportunity to open to the possibility of wealth; it was made to serve as a reminder, a token, a means of expression of that recognition, because that was what we were there to build at the time.

He pulled, from the collection of objects, a small piece of green jade carved into the shape of an infinity sign, and tucked it up against the cow's feet. Wealth tends towards boundlessness, when recognized and acknowledged.

Working with cattle is working with optimism and abundance. Goals go from a sense of absence to a sense of purpose and direction, from the unattainable right now to something that one can choose to take a step towards at almost any time.

Kiya is an Egyptian pagan of reconstructionist bent (devoted particularly to Hathor and Set) and a student of the Anderson Feri Tradition. She works extensively with the magic of the written word and other forms of symbol manipulation, leavened with bits of folk magic, chaos magic, neo-shamanism, and anything that seems interesting, useful, and beautiful. She lives in New England with an assortment of family members, two cats, and a python, where she writes, sculpts, and does laundry.

Vodou Wealth Magic: An Introduction
By Kenaz Filan (Houngan Coquille Du Mer)

Christianity's relationship with money has generally been ambivalent at best. The Son of God came as a humble carpenter and advised, "it is easier for a camel to go through the eye of a needle, than for a rich man to enter into the kingdom of God[8]." Excessive wealth suggested an unhealthy concern with the things of this world. By contrast poverty – particularly humble, honest, hard-working poverty – was a sign of grace. The poor could follow the example of sanctified beggars like Sts. Roch and Lazarus or pious peasants like St. Isadore. Contentment with their earthly lot ensured a place in the world to come. Those who came into money through family or enterprise were encouraged to give generously to the church, buying indulgence for their sin of prosperity.

While this attitude has often been honored more in the breach than the observance, it has colored many of our social prejudices and assumptions. And since Western magic is a product of its society (and has incorporated many orthodox and alternative strains of Christian thought), we should not be surprised to find these preconceptions creeping into our practices.

The same could be said for other antecedents of modern magic. Romanticism gave us "states of nature" and pre-Christian utopias untouched by the taint of civilization. They followed the lead of Jean-Jacques Rousseau, who honored "man in his primitive state, as he is placed by nature at an equal distance from the stupidity of brutes, and the fatal ingenuity of civilised man[9]." In America that was combined with the nature-veneration of philosophers like Thoreau.

> *If you are restricted in your range by poverty, if you cannot buy books and newspapers, for instance, you are but confined to the most significant and vital experiences; you are compelled to deal with the material which yields the most sugar and the most starch. It is life near the bone where it is sweetest...*

---

[8] Matthew 19:24 (KJV)
[9] Jean-Jacques Rousseau. "On the Origin of Inequality: The Second Part." (1754).
http://www.constitution.org/jjr/ineq_04.htm.

Superfluous wealth can buy superfluities only. Money is not required to buy one necessary of the soul. – Henry David Thoreau[10]

This Marxist/Luddite distaste for business was combined later with Eastern asceticism as Theosophy, Vedantism, and other movements brought Buddhist and Hindu ideas of renunciation to Victorian and Edwardian occulture. And since these movements were largely the provenance of the moneyed classes, there was an accompanying disdain for too-obvious ambition. Wealth magic was low sorcery: it showed greed and, worse, showed that the magician needed money.

Where these movements had mixed feelings about wealth, postwar counterculture had open hostility. In 1970, England's Isle of Wight Festival degenerated into a battle between promoters and radicals bemoaning entertainment for profit and demanding a free event. "[I]t began as a beautiful dream but it has got out of control and become a monster," said promoter Ron Foulk in his epitaph for what would prove to be the last festival on Wight for 32 years[11]. He could have been speaking of America, where the summer of love had been replaced by several long hot summers of rioting against "The Establishment" to ensnare the complicity of the faceless grey bourgeoisie. Financial success was a sign of moral turpitude: "working-class cred" was the order of the day.

Vodouisants know that in the end everything is an ancestral tradition: we cannot help but show our roots. Many modern magicians have internalized this cultural disdain for money. Most strains of British traditional witchcraft explicitly prohibit charging for initiations. Many Neopagans go further and forbid charging a client for any magical or spiritual services; some would even condemn using magic to improve one's personal finances (It can lead to selfishness and materialism, you know…). And not surprisingly, many of these people who scorn wealth discover that wealth scorns them back.

Yet historically magic has long been a tool for gain. People went to witches to seek prosperity and success, not spiritual folderol and soothing words. Magicians were judged by their miracles and paid for their skill in producing same. In Haiti, Vodou is not just a religion: it is also a career opportunity. A gift for working with the lwa and

---

[10] Henry David Thoreau. "Walden: Chapter 18(Conclusion)." (1854). http://thoreau.eserver.org/walden18.html

[11] "The Isle of Wight Festival 1970." http://www.ukrockfestivals.com/iow1970menu.html.

satisfying a clientele has made some Houngans and Mambos wealthy and has kept many others in relative prosperity in one of the world's poorest countries.

> *In Cap-Haitien, Haiti's second-largest city, Mayor Michel St. Croix estimates that less than 10% of the city's 800,000 residents have jobs. Thanks to aid from the international community, St. Croix was able to provide 400 street-cleaning jobs which paid $3 a day – a sizeable wage in a country where 76% of the population lives on less than $2 a day[12].*

If we wish to learn about wealth magic, we may want to explore how they have found opportunities for advancement in a place where opportunity is in desperately short supply. A great part of a tradition's magic lies in its way of seeing; there is more power in wisdom than spellcraft. Teaching the ins-and-outs of Vodou practice lies beyond the scope of this article (or, indeed, any book, series, or website). To do Vodou money magic, you must first learn how practitioners view both money and magic. This brief introduction may help you to get an idea of some of the underpinnings of Vodou's philosophy... and of our own.

The Blessings of Poverty, the Blessings of Wealth

Haitian Vodouisants know that poverty doesn't make most people saintly or blessed; it just makes them poor. To renounce worldly goods you must first have them, and fasting is only a virtue when it is voluntary. In Vodou, poverty is a sign of weakness; good fortune is a sign one is favored by *Bondye* (God) and the *lwa*. Vodouisants seek not to accept their condition, but to rise above it: in an intensely competitive environment, they believe Vodou provides an edge which can make the difference between hope and despair or survival and death.

A lack of resources and an overabundance of people ensure that very little is free in Haiti, a fact reflected in Vodou's religious and magical world view. The lwa expect to be paid for their favors and Vodouisants expect to be rewarded -- by their clients and by the spirits -- for their services. Vodouisants have no compunctions about demanding money from the lwa, or withholding their offerings if they

---

[12] Jacqueline Charles. "Smugglers, poverty fuel Haiti exodus." *Miami Herald*, July 8, 2007.

don't get a response. There are clearly delineated expectations which priest, client, and lwa are expected to meet, with little room for excuses on any part.

To survive amidst scarcity requires a community. The *famni* (family) shares resources and closes ranks against outside dangers. In exchange for their protection, the individual pledges loyalty and service to the group. This is true of spiritual relations as well as blood ties (the two being oft entwined in Haiti): the société looks after its members and functions as a support group as well as a religious organization. A similar dynamic holds for the interaction between lwa and servitor. The lwa give special attention to those who give them special attention and tangible rewards to those who make tangible offerings. It is a relationship of mutual need and mutual respect.

Many offer thanksgiving to lwa through parties, or *fets*. These events can be very expensive, involving hired drummers, animal sacrifices, and large quantities of food, drink, and other items, as well as labor and assistance from specially trained practitioners. At fets the community is fed: they also receive their own blessings and contractual obligations from the lwa. By holding impressive *fets*, Houngans and Mambos establish standing among their peers. And in exchange for these *fets* (and/or other ceremonies like marriage or initiation) the lwa look after their followers and provide for their needs.

Others may meet their obligations to the spirit in other ways. Wealthy Haitians may have a *maryaj lwa* (marriage to the spirits) performed privately. By marrying their lwa, they affirm their commitment to the spirits without the stigma many of their peers attach to "primitive superstitions." They put aside a certain number of nights every month to avoid sex and sleep alone: they may also wear discreet jewelry to show their marriage, but they do not make their practices public knowledge[13]. A poor Haitian might save for months to buy Freda a small bottle of perfume or a lacy scarf: they might never have the means to pay for their own *fet*, but still make the best offerings they can. Vodouisants give according to their abilities and hope to receive according to their needs: the lwa abide by this arrangement and will often make accommodations for and with their followers.

If neglected the lwa may take away the Vodouisant's wealth and luck. Conversely, servitors may withhold service from their lwa after a

---

[13] See Kevin Filan, "I Married a Lwa: the Sacred Nuptials of Haitian Vodou."
http://www.widdershins.org/vol9iss8/05.htm.

period of misfortune or signs the spirits has been slacking on their end of the bargain. This may seem disrespectful, but it's in keeping with tradition. Practitioners of Goetic magic (strains of which have influenced many societes in Haiti) coerce demons to do their bidding through negative reinforcement, and J.G. Frazer described how Sicilian Catholics in 1893 responded to a prolonged drought by puttting their saints outside and taking away their ornaments until they brought rain[14]. Ultimately, it comes down to economics: in Haiti even a lwa who will not work will not eat.

Misfortune as Sickness: Vodou as Medicine

Illness... may translate itself in the form of simple injury, accidents, dysfunctions of structure of the individual or of his substructure or organs, dysfunctions of the mind or simply in the form of a total collapse which means a complete disability to function efficiently within oneself, in one's society or in the World. – Houngan Max Beauvoir[15]

Vodou sees luck is a tangible thing, as real as your heartbeat and the breath which flows through your body. Bad luck is like pain, a symptom of something which requires attention and which must be corrected if possible. Platitudes about acceptance and detachment will do nothing to fix the underlying problem: actions will be required. One of the primary roles a Houngan or Mambo plays in the community is healer. They consider the physical, psychic and spiritual causes of dis-ease (almost any variety of misfortune) and act to cure or alleviate that condition. Before doing a money *wanga* (magical working), a Houngan or Mambo might ask questions like: *Does a negative spirit need to be driven away from the client?*

There are innumerable ways by which one might attract a malevolent spirit. A *djab* (untamed spirits) might make its home in a rock or a stump on or near your home. You might move into or near a place which had once been the scene of a violent murder and draw the attention of a *mo* (troubled dead spirit, from the French *mort*). Once they've attached themselves to their host, these parasites can eat luck

---

[14] See J.G. Frazer, *The Golden Bough*, Chapter 5. The Magical Control of the Weather. Section 2. The Magical Control of Rain. http://www.sacred-texts.com/pag/frazer/gb00502.htm.
[15] Max Beauvoir. "Masterly Vodou Medicine & the Spiritual Structure of Man." http://www.vodou.org/masterly.htm.

as well as health and vitality. They will also produce a "creepy" aura which is hardly conducive to running a profitable business or getting promoted at work. If you've been having a run of bad luck, you may have drawn the attention of some spiritual nasty.

Although Vodou has become infamous for "curses," Vodouisants are far more concerned with defense than offense. By combining common substances like salt, holy water, and locally available herbs with prayer, they can create powerful baths that will send most negative spirits scrambling for higher ground. While the composition of those baths is largely oathbound and shared only with students and house members, there are many steps you can take to cleanse and protect yourself. Regular cleansing and banishing rituals, keeping your living and working areas clean and putting up holy symbols and wards – you may well find that good spiritual and magical hygiene is all it takes to improve your financial position. A surprising number of people, especially people with psychic sensitivity, are playing host to parasitic or negative entities.

Has the client offended a spirit? Even the most benevolent or positive entities can wreak havoc if they are crossed. A client who has neglected or broken a promise to the *mistè* (mysteries) will soon find that the spirits can take away everything they have given. Someone who has inadvertently disrespected a shrine or holy place might have a run of serious misfortune. If we accept that magic is real, we must also accept that it can be dangerous, and that our good intentions may have little more impact in the spirit world than in the physical. Vodouisants will seek to repair the damage done by a number of means, ranging from herbal treatments to baths to calling down the lwa and asking them to intervene.

There are also people who are called to account for ancestral debts. A spirit your ten times removed great-grandfather served decides it wants to renew its ties to your family – and make your life miserable until it catches your attention. A spirit may also attach itself to a client at a ceremony or via a magical item; it may accompany the client for years before introducing itself. This is not a curse – quite the opposite, in fact! Once the spirit is propitiated, it will become a great blessing and a powerful protector and friend. But the channels of communication must first be opened, and the offerings must be made.

In this situation, the Houngan or Mambo will act as arbitrators between the spirit and their client. They will seek to ascertain what the lwa want, then try to come to a solution mutually acceptable to both (This is to be contrasted with the "you must bring me nine hundred-dollar bills wrapped around an egg" approach; there's a difference between spirit work and outright fraud). The ancestral spirit might be propitiated by a bottle of rum and the promise of a weekly candle. Ezili Danto might demand a party at which a pig was sacrificed in her name and then eaten by the congregation, while Ghede might be content with a new pair of sunglasses and some piman (peppered rum): the specifics will vary with each person and with each spirit.

If the spirit's demands are excessive, the Vodouisant may say "I am sorry, but you will have to provide me the money first." There is no disrespect in bargaining with the spirits. But we need to keep in mind that the spirit world is not a cornucopia which exists to pour out blessings and knowledge to us. Rather, it is a marketplace where we receive as we give, and a place where our debts can be more onerous than any mortgage or credit card bill. We can say "no" to the spirit – but if we say "yes" we will be held to our promises. Spiritual commitments should not be undertaken lightly and spiritual promises should not be made without careful thought. Before you call on supernatural aid, make sure you are willing to pay the price... because one way or another you will.

What spirits walk with this person? Vodouisants believe that everyone has spirits who walk with them: those who serve their spirits have an advantage over those who do not. This is not a religion where power is reserved to the clergy. While initiation provides a better connection to the lwa and offers protection, there are many people who work with the spirits and see clients without ever setting foot in a *djevo* (initiatory chamber).

Everyone has a *met tet* ("master of the head"), along with other spirits accompanying them through ancestry or for other reasons. Actions (noble or ignoble) can attract the spirits: so can visiting a psychically active place or attending an effective ceremony. Most Houngans and Mambos would spend little time worrying about how you acquired your spirits and concentrate instead on how you might best serve them.

Learning who your spirits are and what is required from each of them is not a question which can be answered by a book. A reading from a skilled professional or a spiritual counselor will prove a useful investment. In the interim, you may find it useful to concentrate your attentions on a few familiar spirits rather than scattering your attentions across eras and pantheons. In matters of importance it is generally best to favor deep and close relationships over shallow and interchangeable ones.

Conclusion

In the end, some might wonder what Vodou has to teach us about wealth magic. Cynics frequently ask "if Vodou is so powerful, why is Haiti the poorest country in the Western hemisphere?" We might turn the question around. Vodou has survived a century of slavery, three centuries of oppression, 19 years of US occupation, and innumerable efforts by state and church (evangelical and Catholic) to eradicate this 'primitive superstition.' Like the Haitian people, Vodou exists in the face of overwhelming odds. Its continued existence is testimony to its power and to the strength of its followers.

Kenaz Filan is the author of *The Haitian Vodou Handbook* and the managing editor of *newWitch* Magazine. Sie resides in the New York metropolitan area, where sie is presently working on several new books.

Green Magick: Money and Pagan Consciousness
By Leni Hester

When it comes to money, many Pagans would benefit from being asked, "What is your major malfunction?" Over the decades I've been in the Craft community, I've noticed that no single issue trips up as many folks, is as persistently challenging on both material and psychic levels, and is as perennially difficult to transform as our personal and collective relationships to money. Even issues of Pagan sexuality, which can be incredibly triggering for many of us, do not provoke the same response. Most Pagans have had to confront issues of sexuality at some point, and there is plenty of support in our community for dealing with issues of discomfort around sexuality and gender. There is far less discussion about money, and as a community we suffer from not turning our attention to it.

The first thing we have to ask about the Pagan relationship to money is how much relevance that question even has. Isn't money too mundane and prosaic to be of interest to us? What does money—that 'filthy lucre'—have to do with us? Part of what Pagan practice encourages us to do is really examine the structures and institutions of our larger culture, critique what we find wanting, and then set about rediscovering or creating structures that serve us and our community better. For so many Pagans, the most compelling part of the Path is waking up from the mass cultural trance of materialism, violence, and consumption that imperils us and entire communities of living things. The pursuit of money as an ultimate goal is highly respected in our society, and many of those who don't subscribe to these "dominator values" get ridiculed and left behind. If money equals power, eschewing the single-minded pursuit of money is almost like consciously accepting powerlessness. It means that in many cases, those of us who don't participate in the competition for ever greater material comfort and more possessions run the risk of getting left behind and ignored. Conversely, many Pagans with good jobs have felt the need to keep silent about their faith, so as not to jeopardize their livelihoods. This is something that keeps Pagans marginalized—that our values are often at odds with the larger community, and that it is at times almost impossible to reconcile our material needs and personal ambition, with our ethics and core values. The real risks and consequences of speaking honestly about this has kept many Pagans silent.

Many religious communities have to answer these questions about worldly possessions and spiritual grace for themselves. These issues are resolved in various ways, from a full-on, unabashed acceptance of materialism and spirituality as fully compatible (i.e. the Christian right elite) to a complete rejection of material values in favor of the spiritual (the Amish, ascetic sects of Buddhism and Hinduism). These questions are particularly salient for Pagans because of the Earth-centeredness of our philosophical and ethical base. How can we live in the world, and yet not be completely worldly? What is the best way for us to live, to achieve, without taking more from our Earth than we give back? These questions continue to arise because they are difficult to answer. Finding the balance seems nearly impossible at times, given our inability to envision what this balance would even look like.

All of this is somewhat ironic because a powerful definition of Witchcraft is the ability to shape reality through will. If so many Pagans are comfortable with picking and choosing the types of work they do, the deities they work with, the parts of the dominant paradigm they choose to play with and the parts they choose to ignore, why is money somehow immune to this level of examination? So many human constructs are up for deconstruction and outright ridicule among Pagans—gender, sexuality, racism, sexism, militarism, monotheism—why is money just kind of taken "as written," almost as if it is a force of nature: unpredictable, arbitrary, cruel, and beyond our abilities to change?

I think that this attitude has really not served Pagans well at all. While money itself could be a symbol of the vast disconnect between our actual lives and the programmed model of how we "should" be living, claiming that money is too mundane and tainted to be worthy of the discerning Pagan eye does us all a disservice, and leads to keeping an unbalanced relationship with money in play. On the one hand, we have the Pagan slacker: perpetually broke, often mooching for support, unwilling to take responsibility for such trivia as bills, debts, or vocation. They allow others to foot the bill while they give themselves pats on the back for being "above it all." Often these people are a drain on the community.

Equally annoying are what I call "Pagan Calvinists." While many Pagans report that becoming Pagan seems to have initiated them into vocational and material success, some folks take this manifestation of right livelihood and living well to a creepily arrogant extreme. They claim their wealth is proof positive of their karmic ascendancy, a reward straight from God Herself, regardless of what they do to get their money or how they spend it. Having money is its own justification, and because they are obviously enlightened, there is no need to scrutinize their purchases or hold them accountable for the choices they make. This has in the past two decades also manifested as the extensive commodification and commercialization of the Craft. There is nothing wrong in buying tools of the Craft. There is nothing wrong in having to replace your supplies of herbs, candles, incenses, wine, etc. Some Witches and Pagans may even pay for training in their various paths. But part of the explosion in Pagan merchandising brings an overweening focus on the material aspects of Craft, which reduces the practice of the Craft into a commodity.

What Pagans must do is end the mystery and embrace a balanced and thoughtful approach to money. What is money, really? Money is just a piece of paper or a metal object, at least on the surface. What is money a symptom of? What does it really represent? Why is it so loaded for us? Because money symbolizes so many things, on so many levels, it is helpful to break it down a bit, to deconstruct its various meanings and how they resonate with our own values. On a material level, money represents our ability to care for ourselves and our loved ones. It represents our labor, our livelihood, and our time, what we are willing to give for what we want and need. It is our work on this earth, our skills, and our talents, and what are we able to do and to give back to our communities. Because money is tied to labor, it is tied to our passions, our vocations, and our talents. It can also carry lots of shame, guilt, and disappointment. None of these are trivial things. Money is intimately linked with our survival on the most basic levels. With such high stakes, it's no surprise it takes on an almost mythic aura.

To help break the taboo, take out a dollar bill out of your wallet or purse, and look at it, really look at it. Feel it between your fingers, smell it, tear a corner off to feel the fibers. Try to use the meditation tool, Beginner's Mind, and pretend you are seeing a dollar bill for the first time ever. Really look at the engravings on it, the words and images, the different colored inks. So much is written on the occult iconography of the dollar—whole movies have been made about it! Check out those stories and see if any of those conspiracy theories tweak your interest. Change your perception of money as just an object, and make room for new perspectives on it to emerge. Remind yourself that much of the time, the money we earn and spend doesn't even appear in our hands as an object, but exists only as numbers on a page, or as electronic impulses in different computer databases. It's dizzying to think of entire rivers of money that cross the planet every day, swirling from continent to continent like massive ocean currents, borne from stock exchange to stock exchange on the rise and fall of 1s and 0s. This too is money, and make no mistake, for many people on this planet these fluctuations of currency and goods spell life and death. To feel impotent in this crushing wave of market demands is natural. Therefore it's even more important that we become consciously aware of this global tide of money. Most of us, however humble our living standards, are probably enormously wealthy compared to the majority of humans with whom we share the planet. We cast a bigger shadow in terms of resources we demand and expect, but we also can exercise greater choice. It is imperative that we spend our global dollar in accordance with our values and our will. We can in fact, vote with our dollar. For some of us this may mean donating to charities or non-profits whose work we admire and want to support. For some of us, this may mean purchasing only organic or locally grown food, or shopping in certain stores while boycotting places like the Gap or Wal-Mart. For some of us, it means living "off the grid" as much as possible, or living without debt. Like the web of life, money manifests as a connection between people and communities, and what happens in one part financially cannot help but affect other parts. As above, so below. We as Pagans see that pattern reiterated again and again, in nature, in our spiritual lives. Why is it surprising to see it manifest in our checkbooks?

In the end, do we want money, or do we want those things and experiences that money can provide for us? Removing the veil of illusion on this fact is helpful in recreating a more conscious relationship with money. Usually, it is not money that we long for when we say we want it, and it's often not money that we're lacking when we lament that we are broke. We desire ease, leisure, travel, material objects, time for family and friends—when I say "I need/want more money," I am usually longing for these things instead. Magickally, it is often easier to manifest the thing we want the money for (a trip, a new car, pick your poison), than to manifest some arbitrary amount of cash. This is because our attachment to our actual desire is more immediate, more material and real, but our deepest self recognizes money as a symbol, a substitute and a stand-in for the real thing. As such it is a tool, a means to an end, not the end itself. It is more neutral and harder to connect to on a soul level.

When I look beneath my desire for money, I find myself longing for certain types of abundance and ease, for a general prosperity that doesn't really have a price tag, just a general sense of there being enough to cover myself and my family, and a bit extra to share or to bank up against the proverbial rainy day. It also means having a financial plan that tends towards the realistic and mindful, that is short on excess and waste, but tried to provide for fun and spontaneity and the occasional splurge, as well as having the rainiest days provided for as well. Those are my goals, and every day I work towards them, and sometimes, often, I slip up.

Now, ask yourself this: What is prosperity for you? Do you see it in your own life? Why or why not? Do you feel prosperous? If not, why? If money is an indication of our abilities to take care of ourselves materially, does feeling perpetually broke and stressed about money serve us spiritually? How far off are we from our financial goals, and why? What can we do to achieve these goals, and why do we choose not to? These are questions each of us has to answer for ourselves.

Managing our money is one of the many responsibilities of adulthood, and deserves as much mindfulness and care as any truly important part of our lives. We don't have to live in money's trance, but we do need to provide for ourselves materially as well as psychically. We are not serving our Gods by neglecting our human needs. Indeed, by managing our finances appropriately, we as Pagans can help others and give back to our communities as well.

In order to foster more abundance, and a deeper awareness of money as a tool and not an enemy, I wrote the following ritual. It was first performed by Beachfyre Coven, in Miami, Florida on Ostara, 2005.

The Bunny Money Ritual

This rite was designed to call upon the multiplying powers of rabbits to aid us in manifesting more abundance in our finances. It fits very well as an Ostara rite, since it utilizes the powers of initiation, increase, and fertility.

Decorate a central altar for prosperity: green cloth, green and gold candles, and burn a prosperity or 'money luck' incense. Use images and projects that symbolize wealth and luxury to you. I've taken my entire "loose change" jar and upended it on the altar, or thrown the coins on the floor. This creates a wonderful feel of excessive riches and abundance. On the altar have a basket with a rabbit image of some kind. I've used bunny rabbit salt and pepper shakers and called upon Mama Bunny and Papa Bunny. My coven used a rabbit-shaped piggy-bank for this, which became the Holder of the Coven Funds thereafter. Rabbit is a sacred animal in many traditions, so calling upon such diverse Goddesses as Gaia, Inanna, and Oestre is in keeping with both the time of year and the energies of abundance and increase. However, I've been able to call upon these energies at other times of the year as well.

Circle up and create sacred space, ground, and center. Call in quarters and deities.

Have attendant each take out a dollar bill.

Meditation: Hold your dollar bill. Feel it between your fingers. Smell it. Look at it. Tear a piece of it. Know that it is not so fearsome; it is only a piece of paper. Breathe. Now think about what abundance means for you. What would prosperity and wealth look like? Our intention is to support and generate abundance and prosperity for ourselves and those we love. What would that look like?

Here coveners can share their needs or plans around abundance. Examples: "I want to finish paying off my student loans." "I wish for a new, more reliable car." "I want to do some renovations to my home." "I want to get out of debt completely." "I want to travel to Europe next summer." Once this round of responses is finished, the meditation resumes:

These dollars that we hold represent those intentions, and as well as our general wishes for prosperity. In asking for abundance, we call the spirit of the Sacred Rabbit to impart to this money hir powers of multiplication and reproduction for our benefit and for the benefit of our families and community.

The basket is passed around and everyone puts their dollar in. The rabbit image(s) is put back on top.

We call on the energies of increase and multiplication to charge up our money. Make all our money able to reproduce, and able to pass along this gift of fertility to all the money it rubs up against. When we deposit into the bank, this dollar will pass along that gift to all the money in there. When we spend it, it will pass along that blessing of abundance to all the money it touches. If we give it to a friend or a worthy cause, that dollar will also 'impregnate' their funds with same reproductive power. In manifesting this abundance, we are aware that we can pass along those blessings to others. Sharing makes all our fortunes grow.

It is good here to raise energy for the money, by chanting, singing or by doing a line dance or a conga around the basket. However it is done, when the energy is high, pull it towards the center, towards the basket with the money. Focus it as the whole group moves in towards it. Further this intention by toning "ohm". Push all that good energy into the cash to charge up the spell. When this is done, pass the basket around widdershins and everyone takes a dollar out (though not necessarily the one they put in). Carry that dollar in your wallet for a few days before spending it, and spend it on something designed to get you closer to your intention for the spell. If you want to pay off debts, deposit it into your checking account and send off a payment. If you want to increase your savings, deposit it into your savings account. If you have a special large purchase you're saving for, spend the dollar on something symbolic of that purchase or throw it into a change jar that's designated for that purpose.

It is also helpful to write your desired outcome on a deposit slip and sealed it in an envelope, to be opened later. This time can be determined by the nature of your spell—maybe a lunation, a season, six months or a year later. Open the envelope and see what you wrote down. Have you achieved it? Honestly evaluate why or why not.

My experience of performing this ritual three times now is that there has been a sustained increase in my fortunes since then, and there's usually a little 'pop' immediately after performing it. Our coven kept the 'bunny-bank' for our coven funds and have never failed to be surprised when we count the contents. Our 'Bunisha' always has more cash than we account for, a wonderful affirmation for our spell.

Leni Hester has been a self-identified Witch since she was 5 years old. In the past 25 years of following the path of Transformational Magick, she has studied Gardnerian & Alexandrian Wicca, the Western Mystery Tradition, yoga, and AfroCuban Santeria (Lucumi). She got her primary magickal training in the Lunatic Fringe. Currently studying Feri Witchcraft and finishing up her Masters in African-American Literature, Leni raises two young daughters with her husband, in Denver, Colorado.

Managing Prosperity through Magic

A Night on the Beach with Yemaya
By Mama Donna Henes, Urban Shaman

Several years ago, I received a rude reality awakening. Suddenly, with no warning, the entire income/financial segment of my life fell apart. Nothing that I had planned and worked for worked out (at least in the short run.). Nothing. Not one damn thing. It was through no fault of my own, or probably any one else's. Whatever the reason, my professional structures collapsed. Everything I scheduled months and years in advance fell through at the very last minute, which resulted in major money trouble. My midlife hormones were all over the place, too, which definitely didn't help matters any.

I was especially upset about the coming Summer Solstice. I had been booked to design and facilitate a large public ceremony for this Celestially Auspicious Occasion in Boulder, Colorado. But, at the last possible second, their plans dissolved and I was left dangling. Since I had planned to be away, I hadn't organized a celebration for my New York City community, either. I was to be Solsticeless.

My frustration surfaced as rarely expressed rage. Instead of exploding, I seethed. Snappish, sarcastic, rude, and nasty, I was sending out negative vibes all over the place, and starting to attract volatility towards myself. Caught on the anger/self pity treadmill, I did nothing to make myself feel better except to work myself mercilessly, trying to reverse my growing debt situation.

As is common for most of us when matters become bleakest, I stopped doing everything that might have helped me to feel better: yoga, tai chi, vitamins, gym. I really hit bottom. I was wound so tight that I wanted to break glass. I craved the catharsis of smashing something to bits, and in the process, the satisfaction of shattering my disappointment, resentment, and fury.

So I started imaging a rage ritual where I could tranceform my anger and make it work for me. Where can one responsibly break glass and not wake, scare, or hurt anyone? Do no damage? A West Indian friend suggested breaking a coconut instead of glass. She urged me to go to the beach and offer seven coins and molasses and coconut to the sea.

She was referring to the rites of Yemaya, the Yoruban orisha of the oceanic source of all life and love, Goddess of Love, Passion, Sensuality, Money, Prosperity, and Abundance. She said that this ritual would break my unlucky cycle in seven days. Rona had no idea just how perfectly apt her instinct was when she suggested I pay Yemaya a visit. She knew that the Summer Solstice is customarily the day to honor Yemaya, but she didn't know that I was in search of a special solstice observance.

So there it was. I would have a private ritual on the beach – just the moon and the sea and me.

The Solstice Ceremony to Honor Yemaya

The day of the solstice started quite auspiciously as my friend Linda, who had come to visit, handed me a bouquet of sunflowers. She asked me if they were all right in that hesitant way that people have when they want to please. Actually, I'm not a sunflower girl ordinarily, but sunflowers on the Summer Solstice couldn't have been more perfect.

At about 2:30 AM of that shortest night of the year, I packed up my canine companion and co-celebrant of a decade's worth of rituals, and a picnic basket full of ritual goodies and drove out to South Beach, Staten Island where I had done many public Winter and Summer Solstice ceremonies over the years.

When I pulled into the lot, I noticed a group of about 30 black figures, all dressed in white coming in from the direction of the beach. Aha! A Yemaya gathering was just dispersing. They must have met at midnight, the traditional time. I parked my car. Then, dressed all in white also, I proceeded out onto the sand to take over the ceremonial late shift. We were celebration cousins crossing in the night.

The beach was deserted except for a young couple some distance from me who were frolicking like fairies in the dark: dancing, hugging, doing what looked like contact improvisation, making love. Again, how perfect. The Summer Solstice is traditionally a mating time. In the distance they were faceless, ageless, genderless, raceless — archetypal silhouettes down the shore looking so pretty; sexy scenery for my ceremony.

That year, the solstice happened to fall on the Full Rose Moon. Which was especially auspicious, as Yemaya is especially fond of white roses. I brought with me an offering bundle containing all of the roses from my two small bushes, which I intended to send out to sea on the receding waves. Chanting in homage to La Luna, I tossed the flowers into the moonlit luminous water, a present of beauty for the Lovely Lady of the Sea who loves romantic presents of champagne, flowers, and sweets.

It didn't take long to realize that the tide was coming in, washing my roses right back to me. My first impulse was to think that She was rejecting my gift. But I later came to understand that She was showing me that the riches, the offerings, the prayers can return to the person making the offering. She was showing me a sign that my problems were going to be solved: That the universe *does* send me what I need. At the time, though, I was clearly too dense and I missed the meaning.

Ever accommodating, She gave me another message, this one too obvious to ignore. Some yards away from the water, up in the dry sand, I spotted an embedded rock with a flat surface. "Go there, use that", She whispered in the wind. So I laid the wet roses retrieved from the surf on this stone altar and added all the rest of the fresh and dried buds and petals from my bag. Carefully, I made my bed of roses.

On top of the roses, I placed seven shiny dimes. Then I poured the jar of molasses around the base of the rock creating a sticky moat, dribbling the last trickle, á la Pollack, over the flowers and coins. And over this entire creation, I sprinkled golden glitter creating a luscious sacred sundae. Seated at my sticky shrine, I chanted my moon chant, "Luna, Lu na na. Lu na na na" until the solstice moment at 4:20AM. When that time came, I offered the coconut.

Right next to the rock tabernacle was a smaller round stone the size of a cantaloupe. I began banging the coconut against this offering stone, bringing it down again and again, finally bashing the whole rock into the sand. It is really hard to break a coconut with a stone. The frustration of trying to break the shell increased with each attempt and mixed with all of my pent up fury. Again and again, I banged away, grunting, yelling, screaming, and then suddenly, finally, I cracked the nut.

I held it up above my head in triumph, showering the altar and myself with sweet, succulent milk. "It's over!" I shouted into the juicy downpour. What an incredible catharsis — ever so much more fulfilling than the mere smashing of glass would have been.

I sat, then, sated. The moon moved down to the horizon. The sky gradually got gray, then blue. The sea washed in and covered my prayers. When my tabernacle rock was completely swallowed, I followed it out into the ocean where I floated on my back and let Yemaya bathe me clean. I drove back home over the Verrazano Bridge just as the sun came up.

Exactly one week after my solstice ceremony, I was packing my purse to go out for a very long walk. I decided to take my travel wallet instead of my normal one, because it is smaller and lighter. When I

91

opened an inside flap I discovered $70 inside. Not $50, not $80, but $70, precisely seven days after I laid down those seven dimes. Fortune, like fury, Yemaya taught me, ebbs and flows with the tides.

Donna Henes, is an internationally renowned urban shaman, award-winning author, popular speaker and workshop leader whose joyful celebrations of celestial events have introduced ancient traditional rituals and contemporary ceremonies to millions of people in more than 100 cities since 1972. Mama Donna, as she is affectionately known, is the author of *The Queen of My Self, The Moon Watcher's Companion, Celestially Auspicious Occasions: Seasons, Cycles, and Celebrations, Dressing Our Wounds In Warm Clothes* and the CD, *Reverence To Her: Mythology, the Matriarchy, & Me.* She writes a weekly column for UPI Religion and Spirituality Forum. In addition to teaching and lecturing worldwide, she maintains a ceremonial center, spirit shop, ritual practice and consultancy in Exotic Brooklyn, New York, Mama Donna's Tea Garden & Healing Haven, where she works with individuals and groups to create personally relevant rituals for all of life's transitions. www.DonnaHenes.net

Ancient Commerce Magick
By Tony Mierzwicki

"The gods help them that help themselves"

Aesop (620–560 BCE), a slave and story-teller who lived in Ancient Greece, is best remembered for his collections of brief stories, titled *Aesop's Fables*. His fables usually involve animals in banal incidents as a tool to convey profound truths. Amongst the pearls of wisdom Aesop left was: "The gods help them that help themselves."

This saying was paraphrased to "God helps them that help themselves" by Benjamin Franklin, whereupon it crept into everyday vernacular. This idea, contrary to the belief of many, does not appear in the Bible. In fact, it extols the importance of spiritual self-reliance, which is inconsistent with Christianity.

Many people resort to magick or prayer in an attempt to acquire wealth, expecting it to drop into their laps. Aesop's advice was to meet the gods halfway, which in this case implies being proactive in wealth acquisition. In ancient times, there were no stock markets, banks or other institutions offering investment portfolios. In ancient times, many who were serious about wealth acquisition resorted to commerce magick.

Ganesha and Contemporary Commerce Magick in the East

India has a continuous tradition of polytheistic practice, whereas pagans in the Western world are struggling to undo 1500 years of Christian suppression in their quest to rediscover their gods. There are valuable lessons to be learned from India regarding folk magick – how ordinary people interact with their gods in a practical everyday sense. These lessons are relevant for pagans in the Western world. It is pertinent to examine how the gods help those who help themselves in contemporary India.

The most widely worshipped god in India is Ganesha. Ganesha is the principal deity associated with traders and merchants and was spread by them throughout much of West and South Asia from approximately the tenth century onwards. Portrayed as an elephant headed man with a protruding belly, Ganesha is venerated as the lord of beginnings, patron of the arts and sciences, and the god of intellect and wisdom. The merchant community provides the earliest inscription invoking Ganesha before any other deity. These days, Hindus of all sects will invoke him at the beginning of any important undertaking, including business, rituals or ceremonies. His image is found in countless Hindu owned business establishments and shops. Hindu businessmen seek his blessings each morning before work. Hindu taxi drivers set up altars on their dashboards dedicated to Ganesha.

Not surprisingly, pagans in the pre-Christian world venerated a god with many similar attributes to Ganesha as part of their commerce magick, and this god was Hermês.

Hermês and Thoth

Legend has it that the Greek god, Hermês (known as Mercury to the Romans), was the son of Zeus and Maia. Zeus was the supreme god in the Greek pantheon, uniting in himself all the attributes of divinity – he was omnipotent, all-seeing and all-knowing. Maia was a Naiad (nymph) and the daughter of Atlas (the god who bears the heavens upon his shoulders).

Hermês was born one morning in the fourth month on Mount Cyllene in Arcadia. He invented the lyre by noon, stole fifty head of cattle from his brother Apollô which he hid in a cave, and returned to his crib. Apollô by means of his prophetic power, divined that Hermês was responsible and took him before Zeus. Hermês so impressed Apollô with his playing of the lyre, that in exchange for the lyre, Apollô allowed Hermês to keep the cattle and gifted him the golden staff of fortune and riches, and with some small ability in divination and prophecy. Zeus made Hermês herald to the gods and guide of the souls of the dead into the afterlife. Hermês' attributes are seen here as inventiveness, versatility, trickery, and cunning.

In his birthplace, Arcadia, Hermês was seen as a god who ensured the fertility of pastures and herds. Elsewhere, he was a god of crops, as well as mining and seeking buried treasure. Hermês was a god of roads and a patron of travellers. As travel was normally engaged in for trading, Hermês became associated with commerce, and hence profit. The idea of profit was then extended to include thievery, trickery, and games of chance. Successful trading requires good communication skills and so this also became the province of Hermês.

The cult of Hermês began in his birthplace in Arcadia and then spread throughout Greece. The Agora (marketplace) was an essential part of each ancient Greek city-state. One of the epithets of Hermês was Agoraios (of the Market-place), in keeping with his role as patron of commerce. There were statues of Hermês Agoraios within Southern Greece in Elis, Athenai (Athens) in Attika, Sikyon in Sikyonia, Sparta in Lakedaimonia, and Pharai Town in Akhaia; as well as within Central Greece in Thebes in Boiotia. The best known Agora was the one located in Athens, and many graffito dedications to Hermês have been found there.

As Hermês was born in the fourth month, the number four was sacred to him. In Athens he was honoured with sacrifices on the fourth of every month. The sacrifices offered to Hermês consisted of incense, honey and cakes; while non-vegetarians had the option of including pigs, lambs and young goats. The ancient manner of sacrifice involved burning incense with wheat which had been kneaded with honey on altars, placing twigs of olive wood on those altars, and using wine for a libation (This manner of sacrifice was used for a number of deities including Hermês).

The various characteristics associated with Hermês made him well suited to a role as the messenger of the gods, a task that he carried out with great diplomacy and tact. In this role, he was associated with learning, mental and physical agility, and was honoured by athletes. In later times, Hermês became known as the inventor of writing, mathematics, astronomy and music. He was generally thought of as the archetypal magickian. He was the god of sleep and dreams.

The earliest representations of Hermês were of a mature man with long beard and long hair. Later he was portrayed as a young athletic runner, wearing a round winged hat and winged sandals. He carried the caduceus (kerykeion), a long staff around which two serpents were entwined, symbolising good health and healing. The image of two copulating serpents was actually borrowed from ancient Near Eastern tradition.

The famous Swiss psychologist, Carl Gustav Jung (26 July 1875 – 6 June 1961), made many notable contributions to the study of mysticism, sociology, literature, and the arts, including the concept of the psychological archetype. Many students of the occult explain the striking similarities between the deities of various cultures by claiming that they are based on the same archetypal energies or forces. Historically, the equating of various deities probably began with the Greeks, who described foreign deities in terms of their own.

95

In Egypt, the Greeks identified Hermês with Thoth. Thoth was the scribe of the gods. He had complete knowledge and wisdom; he invented all the arts and sciences. Thoth was represented in two forms – the sacred ibis (*Threskiornis aethiopicus*) and the dog-faced baboon (*Papio cynocephalus*). He was depicted as these appear in nature, or in the case of the ibis, anthropomorphic with the bird's head.

Hermês and Ancient Commerce Magick in the West

It is important to note that the number of spells which survived the pious burnings of magickal books instigated by the founding fathers of the Christian church is very small. As an example, when St Paul was in Ephesus:

"Many of them also which used curious arts brought their books together, and burned them before all men: and they counted the price of them, and found it fifty thousand pieces of silver." [Acts 19:19, King James Bible]

Thus, to develop an accurate comprehensive picture of ancient magickal practices is akin to attempting to discerning the picture within a jigsaw puzzle where most of the pieces are missing. There is always an element of uncertainty, especially within the details.

In my book on Graeco-Egyptian Magick (Mierzwicki 2006), I link a number of spells together in order to create a lengthy invocation to Hermês. A number of these spells involve the construction of a statue of Hermês which is placed within a shop to increase business. It is quite plausible that there were numerous similar spells to increase business that are now lost to us. I am inclined to believe that statues of Hermês in shops of the ancient Mediterranean world were just as prevalent as effigies of Ganesha in contemporary Hindu owned shops.

Readers wanting to recreate one of the specific spells employing a statue of Hermês to increase business in a shop are referred to my book on Graeco-Egyptian Magick (Mierzwicki, 2006), or to the source texts on which it is based. In this article, I analyse the elements of commonality in these spells in order to derive a generic spell.

PGM VIII. 1–63

This spell begins with a long invocation to be made to Hermês and Thoth. An important component of the spell involves the magickian demonstrating his knowledge of Hermês, which includes the statement: "Your plant is the grape which is the olive. I also know your wood: ebony."

A statue of Thoth, the Egyptian Hermês, is then carved out of olive wood (*Olea europaea*). Here the magickian uses the plant aspected to Thoth-Hermês to forge a link between the god and his statue. As stated above, olive wood was used in ancient sacrifices to the gods. The statue should represent Thoth as a small dog-faced baboon sitting down, wearing the winged helmet of Hermês, and with a box on his back (This blending of classical Greek and Egyptian representations of Hermês and Thoth is characteristic of the Hellenistic period. Roman elements in some cases were also incorporated.).

Placed within the box on the baboon's back is a strip of papyrus on which is written the name of Hermês, a number of words of power, and a request to bring business and prosperity to the shop. The carved statue is then left in the middle of the shop. Incense should be burned, so as to ensure profitable business.

It is pertinent to digress and to consider the significance of ebony (*Diospyros ebenum*), a hard dense black wood, carved pieces of which have been found in ancient Egyptian tombs.

Apulieus (123 CE -170 CE) was a philosopher, orator, thaumaturgus (miracle worker), and priest of Asklepius (God of healing and medicine), as well as of Isis and Osiris. He is best remembered for writing "*Asinus Aureus*" ["*The Golden Ass*" or "*Metamorphoses*"], which includes the legend of Cupid and Psyche, examples of the practice of magick and witchcraft, as well as an account of an initiation into the mysteries of Isis.

In 158 CE, Apuleius married a wealthy widow named Pudentilla, who died shortly afterwards. As a result, he was accused of being a magickian who had used witchcraft to win the heart of Pudentilla, by her relatives who coveted her wealth. Apuleius' speech from his trial in Sabrata has been preserved as "*De Magia*" ["*A Discourse on Magic*," also known as "*Apologia*" or "*The Defence*"]. This speech gives much insight into what was believed to constitute magickal practice. Amongst these insights was an accusation that Apuleius had a statue of Mercury (Hermês) carved from ebony, "the most carefully chosen wood," for the sake of "secret, evil black magic..." Apuleius responded that he merely wished to have his statue carved from a "rarer and more durable material." The inference was that ebony was considered the most appropriate material for Hermês for magickal purposes.

PGM IV. 2359–72

This spell does not provide an invocation. The instruction provided is to mix orange beeswax[16], the juice of the aeria plant (perhaps the flowery aeria, *Fumaria officinalis?*) and ground ivy (*Glechoma hederacea*). From this mixture a figure of Hermês should be fashioned, where he is grasping in his left hand a herald's wand and in his right a small bag. A herald's wand was a short wand held by messengers which gave them the authority to speak; it consisted of three shoots, one of which formed the handle, the other two being knotted at the top; the knot was later replaced by serpents to form the caduceus (kerykeion).

A hollow base should be left in the statue. A strip of papyrus with words of power should be placed in the hollow base of the statue. The hollow should then be sealed with more of the beeswax mixture. The statue should then be placed inconspicuously in a wall. A lamp should be lit before the statue, and offerings should be made, so as to bring continuous business to a shop.

PGM IV. 2373–2440

The instruction for this spell states that the figure should be constructed and consecrated during the new moon. Out of unheated beeswax a man should be fashioned dressed in a girdle, with his right hand in the position of begging, and in his left hand a bag and a staff. The staff should have a coiled snake around it, to symbolize the caduceus, and the man should be standing on a sphere that has a coiled snake. The coiled snake is identified with Agathos Daimôn (Agathodaimôn or Good Daimôn – the serpent god who served as the protector of Alexandria).

The statue should be placed into a single block of hollowed-out juniper, with an asp covering the top. Regarding the choice of juniper, Pausanias in his second century CE "Guide to Greece - Greek Geography," wrote that images of deities were normally carved out of ebony, cypress, cedar, oak, yew, and lotus. However, in the dilapidated temple of Hermes Kyllenios on top of Mt Kyllene, the highest mountain in Arkadia, his image was carved of juniper wood, and stood eight feet high.

The spell includes a number of words of power to be inscribed on strips of papyrus and attached to various parts of the anatomy of

---

[16] I concluded that the colour aspected to Hermês was orange in my book on Graeco-Egyptian Magick (Mierzwicki 2006).

the statue. These words of power are to be repeated four times. The statue should then be placed somewhere high within the shop. A sacrifice of incense is offered to the statue, and a short spell is recited, so as to bring business, wealth, and success.

PGM V. 370–446

This spell is actually meant to cause a dream where Hermês appears and prophesies. I am including it as it details the construction of a figure of Hermês.

This spell instructs that a figure of Hermês should be made out of dough consisting of the liquid of an ibis egg (the ibis is connected with Thoth, and hence by extension, Hermês) mixed with a number of plant materials. The plant materials are 28 leaves from a pithy laurel tree (bay laurel tree – *Laurus nobilis*), virgin earth (unploughed), wormwood seed (*Artemisia absinthium* or *Artemesia pontica*), wheat meal (unsifted coarsely ground wheat grain – *Triticum* species) and the herb calf's-snout (unknown, but used in a small number of spells). A variation substitutes 28 new sprouts from an olive tree (*Olea europaea*). Note that the spell *PGM* VIII. 1–63 stated that the olive was aspected to Hermês.

Hermês is to be portrayed wearing a mantle and holding a herald's staff. The figure is placed in a lime wood shrine. Lime wood (*Tilia* species) was often used for carving because of its softness. To use the spell, an invocation is recited and a combination of incense, earth from a grain-bearing field and a lump of rock salt, is burnt. It is important to not talk to anyone during the procedure.

Analysis of Similarities Between Hermês Spells

In each of the spells, a statue of Hermês or Thoth with Hermês attributes is constructed.

Each of these statues and/or their shrines (if required) use construction materials of which at least one is aspected to Hermês. This can be either olive, ebony, or juniper wood, something orange (like orange beeswax), or the contents of an ibis egg (if available). While ebony would appear to be the most appropriate material, its hardness would limit its usage to skilled wood carvers, or those sufficiently wealthy to commission a skilled wood carver. Beeswax or dough are far easier fashion.

Hermês is portrayed as holding a herald's wand or staff, usually in his left hand. This is thus the caduceus (kerykeion) or its predecessor – the herald's wand. Hermês is sometimes portrayed with a bag, which can be in either hand.

Words of power, and sometimes a request to bring business and prosperity, should be attached to the statue. In the examples cited, this is done either by insertion into the base, placement within a box that is part of the statue, or written on strips of papyrus attached to part of the statue. Each of these statues is placed within the shop where commerce is to be improved, either prominently or hidden.

An invocation should be made as part of the consecration procedure. In one case, the invocation is also made prior to preparation of the statue. An unspecified incense should be burned. In one case, the incense is combined with earth from a grain-bearing field and a lump of rock salt. Sometimes an offering is made. An offering is effectively an expression of gratitude to Hermês for, or in anticipation of, an increase in business.

A Generic Commerce Spell Using Hermês

A statue of Hermês should be either made or procured. Fashioning your own statue has the advantage of infusing it with your own energy. Those who either don't have the ability or the time to fashion a statue should procure one which appeals to them and intuitively captures the essence of Hermês.

As a minimum, the statue should include the caduceus (kerykeion). If possible, the statue should incorporate materials aspected to Hermês, as outlined in the spells considered. As a suggestion, a simple ebony base placed under a commercially made statue of Hermês could possibly increase its effectiveness.

Words of power, and sometimes a request to bring business and prosperity, should be attached to the statue. Including the name, Hermês Agoraios, and a request to improve business, would keep the focus of the statue on the commerce aspects of Hermês.

While the spells considered require the burning of incense, the specific incense is not actually identified. In my book on Graeco-Egyptian Magick (Mierzwicki 2006), I identified the incense attributed to Hermês as cassia or kasia (Cinnamomum cassia)[17].

In Athens, at least, Hermês was was honoured with sacrifices on the fourth of every month. However, the calendar in ancient Greece was lunisolar [having twelve months with a periodic intercalation of a thirteenth], but varied in its details in the various city

---

[17] Most of the cinnamon sold in North America is actually cassia.

100

states. Also, the calendar in ancient Egypt had no lunar link, but had 12 months of 30 days, along with five epagomenal (extra) days. This absence of a uniform standard month suggests that it would perhaps be easiest to use the current calendar, and honour Hermês on the fourth day of every month.

How exactly Hermês should be honoured, is a matter of taste and intuition. At the very least, I would suggest a small statue before which one, or perhaps four, orange candle(s) and cassia incense are burned. A hymn should be recited in his honour. The choice is again individual, but Orphic Hymn XXVII: To Hermês, includes pertinent lines:

"Of care the loosener, and the source of gain.
Whose hand contains of blameless peace the rod,
Corucian, blessed, profitable God"

While a short daily veneration to Hermês is appropriate, a more elaborate rite should be practiced on the fourth of every month.

Developing a Successful Business

This essay began with Aesop's statement: "The gods help them that help themselves."

So far, the god appropriate for commerce has been identified, and a method for requesting his help has been outlined. Now, all that remains is for potential entrepreneurs to "help themselves."

The basics of developing a successful business have outlined in numerous publications and websites, and need not be detailed here. It is however, essential to identify a niche for a business idea that is either better, cheaper, or different than existing ones. It is then necessary to develop a business plan and implement it. The whole endeavour is a constant learning process, the assistance for which also comes from Hermês.

Meet Hermês halfway by implementing a prudent business plan and offerning him regular devotions. He will surely reward your efforts.

Bibliography

Atsma, A. (2000-2006). *Theoi Project: Guide to Greek Mythology.* http://www.theoi.com/

Betz, H D (ed.). (1986). *The Greek Magical Papyri in Translation*. Chicago: The University of Chicago Press.

Boylan, P. (1987). *Thoth: The Hermes of Egypt*. Chicago: Ares Publishers Inc.

Burkert, W. (2000). *Greek Religion*. Oxford: Blackwell Publishers Ltd.

Evelyn-White, H G. (2000). *Hesiod, Homeric Hymns, Epic Cycle, Homerica*. Cambridge: Harvard University Press.

Evslin, B. (1975). *Gods Demigods & Demons*. An Encyclopedia of Greek Mythology. New York: Scholastic Book Services.

Faraone, C A & Obbink, D (ed.). (1997). *Magika Hiera: Ancient Greek Magic & Religion*. New York: Oxford University Press.

Fowden, G. (1986). *The Egyptian Hermes: A Historical Approach to the Late Pagan Mind*. Princeton: Princeton University Press.

Godwin, D. (1992). *Light in Extension: Greek Magic from Homer to Modern Times*. St Paul: Llewellyn Publications.

Graf, F. (1999). *Magic in the Ancient World*. Cambridge: Harvard University Press.

Grant, F C (ed.). (1953). *Hellenistic Religions*. Indianapolis: Bobbs-Merrill Company Inc.

Guirand, F. (1986). *New Larouse Encyclopedia of Mythology*. Twickenham: Hamlyn Publishing.

Harvey, P. (1986). *The Oxford Companion to Classical Literature*. Oxford: Oxford University Press.

Kerenyi, C. (1979). *The Gods of the Greeks*. London: Thames and Hudson.

Kerenyi, K. (1976). *Hermes: Guide of Souls*. Putnam: Spring Publications.

Kirk, G S. (1985). *The Nature of Greek Myths*. Harmondsworth: Penguin Books Ltd.

March, J. (2000). *Dictionary of Classical Mythology*. London: Cassell.

Mierzwicki, T. (2006). *Graeco-Egyptian Magick: Everyday Empowerment*. Stafford: Megalithica Books.

Nilsson, M P. (1961), *Greek Folk Religion*. New York: Harper Torchbooks, 1961.

Sanyal, S. *Ganesha*. In *Encyclopedia Mythica*. http://www.pantheon.org/articles/g/ganesha.html

Seyffert, O. (1960). *Dictionary of Classical Antiquities*. New York: Meridian Books Inc.

Taylor, T. (1981). *The Hymns of Orpheus*. Los Angeles: The Philosophical Research Society Inc.

Wikipedia (various articles). http://en.wikipedia.org/

Tony Mierzwicki runs workshops and rituals in Australia and the United States which recreate ancient magickal practices, and include *The Magick of Alexandria* series. He is the author of *Graeco-Egyptian Magick: Everyday Empowerment*, the forthcoming *Alien Magick: Exploring the UFO Phenomenon*, as well as numerous magazine articles, reviews and anthology contributions. Tony has completed three degrees at the University of Sydney – Master of Arts, Bachelor of Engineering and Bachelor of Science.

Vision and the Wealth Quest
by Frater Andrieh Vitimus

Wealth or prosperity magic is often one of the most difficult practices of magic for aspiring magicians to be successful with. Wealth magic is not the same as money magic. Money is often thought of as something below contempt in the artistic/magician crowd. There is a great deal of historical and cultural reasons for this. There are not many wealthy magician/occultist role-models that are public and if the extremely monetarily blessed (as in millionaires) are employing the philosophies and techniques of magic, they are not letting people know how they are doing it (for good reason).

First, does a certain amount of money equal wealth? In Haiti, if I had the normal salary I make in America, I would be a rich land Baron. Let me repeat, wealth is not the same as money. David Lee states, "Money is like the planetary spirit, and Wealth is an aspect of god." I define wealth as the ability and means to do as one desires. By desire, I want to specify that I mean long term desires, as opposed to a passing or fleeting fancy. Wealth is not the ability to arbitrarily spend money; wealth is the idea of living a life that brings happiness by virtue of doing what you want to do. Money is obviously a part of that equation but it is by no means the whole equation of wealth. Equally important to me is the freedom to do what you want to do, because of the surge in happiness and wellness that brings.

Defined this way, I will focus on several points which leap out to me. First, the aspiring magician has to know themselves above all, and be able to formulate a vision or idea of where they want to be. This isn't always possible if a person is in a negative place. Second, money cannot be the end goal. It is one of the means to that end goal, making it extraordinarily similar to food, air, and water in terms of providing a means to those end goals. Third, most people have limiting beliefs and self-restrictions in relation to money. These learned beliefs restrict their ability to retrieve money to fuel their goals. Finally, wealth acquisition must be a process of internal and external manipulations.

While I am not an extremely monetarily blessed individual yet, I have come a far way from being homeless using these ideas and I will become financially, independently wealthy within two years.

Knowing Yourself and Vision

Many magical articles start with the idea of knowing oneself in some way. This phrase is an often abused phrase. It's horribly convoluted depending on which system you are working within. A simpler way to approach knowing yourself is to simply know what you are passionate about and what you like to do. Automatically people assume certain "careers" are money making opportunities. I, myself, fell into this trap with information technologies. I enjoy computer work about 10 hours a week. That's my threshold for enjoying it. That aside, I have a plan and vision for where I want to go. Many lawyers make tremendous amounts of money, but if you do not like arguing the law, this is a tremendously tedious job that requires much research. Most of the reading material is probably not on the New York Times list of exciting books. It's a career that requires a heroic number of hours. I know someone else in Columbus who makes candles. His candles are fantastic for rituals and generally extremely well made for aromatherapy. He has customers in Europe and America and loves what he does. Who is wealthy?

So what do you, the reader, like to do? What are you passionate about? What do you enjoy? Sit down and make a list of the 20 things that you actually like to do. As you are going through that list, make sure to write a paragraph or two on why you like or are passionate about each thing on the list. How much of your current situations match this list? Many new age and abundance philosophers would point out that not many of us work in situations that match our list of passions or even what we like to do. You are not alone by any stretch of the imagination. When you look at list of passions and activities, do any stand out as a really strong or a high priority passion? Now, let me ask you another question; how many things on this list do you think could generate income for you?

For the majority of people, the list probably got a lot shorter and possibly down to nothing. If you did research on Google and through public records, I guarantee there are successful financial examples of each and every one of the things on the list that you like to do. Do a Google search and then correlate the results to the tax records of various businesses. The belief that you can not make money at things you like to do is a self-limiting belief instilled into our collective consciousnesses by our culture. I like to refer to that belief as "the money prison belief".

50 Ft Tall Game:

Let's take on the belief that you are an all powerful magician. Ross Jefferies (1997) has an interesting technique which we can modify. Close your eyes and relax, going deeper and deeper into trance for a few minutes. *Self-hypnosis: The Complete Manual for Health and Self-Change* has some tremendous exercises for self-relaxation if you have not practiced those techniques yet. Perform a banishing or centering ritual. Envision yourself as 50 feet tall with a booming loud voice with complete confidence (you are 50 ft tall, nothing can stop you or worry you). Relax completely. Try to see, hear, and feel all the details of your 50 ft tall romp. As you breathe deeply, imagine with as many senses as you can that you can turn anything you want to gold. For this to be effective, you will need to be in a deeper trance state. Change a few things to gold in the session. You are that unstoppable 50 ft magician with the golden touch. Gently open your eyes, but stay in the mindset of the 50 ft tall unstoppable magician or witch. When you look at your list of what passions and things you like to do, imagine that you can turn any of the results of the passions to solid gold. If you stop yourself, and say you "can't", simply repeat the above exercise attempting to go deeper into trance. Tell yourself, with increasing intensity, that you can do anything. Keep doing this exercise until you can look at your list and know that everything on your list can be turned to gold. What things on list jump out at you the most after doing this exercise?

Suspending the "money prison" belief enough to start working on a different future is not an easy step. The ideas of scarcity and privilege are so ingrained in our thinking that it may be difficult to even dream. The words "I Can't" are so reinforced that most people can't break out of the limitations they impose on themselves. A prison does not need to have walls.

Many of my in-person classes start with methods to create a clear separation between the work "life" and the rest of the person's life. Working at a job that is not enjoyable does have a negative effect on self-esteem. Essentially, the job can eat the emotional reserves of the person doing the work, creating internal conflicts of self-resentment (feeling like you are wasting your time, and not moving on), self-destructive tendencies (staying with the job until you can not take it and then quitting), high stress, and low energy reserves. The body is great at reacting to difficult situations and responds to the demands by producing adrenaline and other stress hormones. Over time, this wears away on the person's ability to optimally function.

There is no energy for outside of work dreams. In a sense, the person feels trapped by the job because they "need" the money, and at the same time, they hate the position (and themselves for being stuck in the situation). The angrier, more stressed, or frustrated a person becomes, the more energy people spend thinking about the situation. I know all too well how this feels. I am sure you, the reader, can relate this to a time in your life as well.

If you have trouble making a list of dreams, we have to break you out of the money prison attitude and the doldrums of any current situation enough to at least dream a little. A simple technique, regardless of how difficult your financial situation is, is simply to schedule time to laugh (Goodheart 1994). While changing the situation may take time, your reaction to your current situation is entirely under your control. Set aside time each day to laugh for 30 minutes. Laugh out loud. At first, you might read that and feel very self-conscious or that the idea is dumb, but once you get started it is really easy to keep laughing. If you have trouble laughing, think of a time when you where laughing. Can you remember what caused the laughter? Or how the laughter feels? Usually, remembering the laughter is sufficient to cause me to chuckle a little and if I keep going back to a memory, I will start laughing out loud. The perfect time to go back to your list of dreams is after laughing for 30 minutes.

Laughing before working on the list of dreams or your own financial magic serves at least two purposes. First, laughter, as Peter Carroll notes, is a banishing and helps clear away negativity around the person (Carroll 1987). Secondly, the combination starts to associate prosperity, money, and wealth with mirth, joviality, and fun. Manifesting your wealth vision must become linked to fun (as opposed to being a prison) or successful results will be more difficult in wealth magic. We all have a lot of baggage to get through regarding money and wealth. The laughter meditation has the additional benefit of breaking down the status quo. Laughter produces a set of endorphins and that happy feeling. The magical adventurer can look at him or herself better because the good feeling allows some detachment even when looking at troubling parts and attitudes of themselves. Starting any long-term magical work from a position of desperation is not the route to long-term success. Simply put, if you are desperate, solutions might work in the short term, but the mindset is not about long-term success. I am not recommending doing nothing about a bad situation, just control your state of mind while you work out of the situation. Adding morning and evening banishing are helpful to pull yourself out of the desperate situation mindset. For me, getting past the immediate situation is often the hardest part of the equation since there is so much motivation to get out of the situation. In a way, this is a type of natural desire of result as explained by Peter Carroll (1987). Once we can see a few dreams that lead out of the situation at hand, we are ready to start manifesting that vision.

Vision and the Wealth Manifestation Process

If you read the material on abundance from Joe Vitale or watch *The Secret* a few times, there is a deluge of opinion that generating wealth is so simple that anyone could do it. The truth is that most people aren't generating wealth (or even money), so the metaphysical presentation of wealth generation as trivial and easy is misleading at best. At worst, this attitude causes many people to turn their frustration on themselves if they do not see the success they are looking for. Manifesting a vision takes sacrifice, but sometimes the sacrifice is only a sacrifice of your own limitations.

Look over each item on your list of favorite visions, and see which items make you the happiest. Consider each item separately. Relax thoroughly, banish or laugh for a longer time, and then imagine yourself 10 years in the future, living the completed vision entirely, profitably, and successfully. How does the future success makes you feel? Many people may already have a dream they would love to live. For now, live it and love it. If you have more then one thing on your list, try each one out. The future isn't set, so mentally explore the possibilities. Note any unexpected parts of the vision, feelings, opinions, and states of mind that occur in you when you are imagining this future possibility.

If you consider your present situation extremely unfavorable, I would recommend doing the laughter meditation (and extra banishing) for a couple of weeks before trying this exercise. When I have done this exercise myself, I am trying to break the emotional hold a situation has over me so that when I am planning for the future, it isn't an echo of the past. If you are only reacting to the set of situations around you, in some ways you are only mirroring that situation and your magical results tend to echo that past.

At this point, perform a divination on each of the possible visions that made you feel good when you imagined completing them. I highly recommend going into a deep trance state before using a divination tool for this purpose. Record your interpretations of the divination. You can keep all of the visions, but we are going to work on the vision that produces the best combination between the

109

divination and the feelings of wellness and happiness that came from living the vision.

The idea of committing to one thing will not be a permanent part of the process, but it is needed early on. A single vision allows the aspiring magician to act in a strategic manner towards their wealth goals and teaches the subconscious the art of manifestation. There are examples in the world of other people doing what you want to do and generating wealth with what they are doing, but they had to stay focused on their goal to achieve that wealth.

The Vision is Nice, But...

An idea of working and doing something you love as your career might be a fun fantasy, but if you don't do anything to manifest it, it is a fantasy which actually can contribute to financial difficulties. To me, this is where Joe Vitale's books and some of the notions in the *The Secret* are misleading. Generating wealth takes commitment, self-modification, research, and having a little luck. We are magicians, witches, and shamans, so we can generate that luck. If your subconscious mind understands your fantasy and then understands that you are not doing anything about manifesting your vision, the mixed messages hinder your magical progression towards the goal. Similarly, many money spells can work, but they are not a progression towards wealth for a similar reason. I can do a money spell, and end up getting a side contract doing something I don't want to do. Likewise, I could get results from a gambling spell but now I have associated money with fickle games of chance. Taking the easiest route to manifestation, the spells were successful money spells, but I have not helped myself associate money with mirth, joy, and happiness in a long term way. In essence, I have successfully acquired money but haven't started the process of building wealth for myself.

Let's refine our vision a slight bit. Imagine yourself doing what you love to do (which 5-10 years out, you were immensely successful at) and at the same time imagine that you have all the physical things you want. An artist can have fine leather furniture, a nice car, and a writer can have a fine Imac G5 20 inch screen with swivel base on an Igo desk attached to a Bose Wavesystem II. While you are doing the things you love, if you have trouble seeing yourself with the physical things and lifestyle you desire, go back to the 50 ft magician exercise and repeat it until you feel the confidence to envision anything you want. Relax into a deeper trance and see yourself doing what you love as the 50 ft magician who, as they are doing what they love to do, can just look at what they are producing (or the transitions they are making) and see each one turn to gold. It's a vision and a dream. Shoot for the stars and you might just get there.

Once we have this nice vision, we have to start to make the vision somewhat more "real". A vision is a bit more encompassing then a specific goal, but we can use an NLP technique to flesh out the vision. Focusing from where you are right now and then imagining yourself moving toward your own vision is a flawed process. First, our impression of what we can accomplish in a short period of time is often far greater then our ability to carry out the tasks. It is easy to skip steps, think wishfully, and generally delude ourselves. NLP, cognitive scientists, and psychologists would agree that it is more effective to instead start at the completion of the vision and work backwards. The vision can be broken down into a series of "long-term" goals. For each goal, ask "What conditions must be in place for this to be able to happen?" Then ask the same question for each condition working backwards through time until you arrive at the very step you have to take right now. Each step should be small enough that you are sure you could succeed at each step forward (Andreas, 1994).

After you have one pathway, redo the exercise on a different day. See how many different sets of steps you could take to produce the vision (chances are good that there is nearly an infinite amount). The different combination of possibilities has the added bonus of helping both the unconscious mind and conscious mind see that your vision is very possible. Many people dream big, but then fail to take the needed steps to manifest their vision. This procedure grounds the vision in actionable steps and tells your unconscious mind, Holy Guardian Angel, Ori, or whatever you want to call it that your dreams are not merely fantasies. Of course, failing to act after you have a plan will not help you gain momentum. Essentially, the magical you hears the underlying message of your physical actions. You, the reader, have to do everything in your power to make sure that each step is a grand and FUN adventure or else the process becomes a chore. Once you take the time to write out the various sets of steps that you need to take, you are, in a sense, taking responsibility for making those steps.

Of course, for each series of steps, we can use divination to get a sense what the issues are internally and externally for that step to be made. Divining across multiple concurrent steps will give you a sense of what is the path of least resistance within the options you discovered for yourself and can give you information about unexpected events. Divinations within the context of the vision again allow you to look at patterns and preempt blocks in the road through magical operations or mundane work. Earlier in the article, I defined wealth as the ability to do what you want in the long term. Setting a long-term plan for a vision allows you to change the context of your magical work. Money spells are not cast out of desperation (which again links money to NEED), but are cast in line with a greater vision where you are doing what you want to do and are happy. If you are working towards your own happiness and wealth, you will be surprised at how much joy the process brings.

One technique I use is to go back to the vision fully with all of the senses. Spending time in the vision should make you happy and it should be a fun place to be. Then, while in the happy and fun place, I use a sigil or other enchantment to ease my transition into the next step on my list (if this is needed). 30 minutes of laughter will also bring most people to a fun and happy mental state. The process of divination can save you some time. If you had to do a magical operation for each step in the process, the whole journey would be tedious and tiresome. In some cases, a money or income spell will be needed to make a transition step since money, like air, is a needed component to move around goods. Each ritual done for this greater purpose should be done while in an ecstatic and happy state of mind. Make rituals you are doing in line with the purpose as fun as you can imagine (because the end goal, that vision, will be fun). Wealth is not money. We want the far greater prize of being able to do what we like while living how we like. Peter Carroll in *Liber Null* and *Psychonaut* details the process of sigilization (Carroll, 1987), although other forms of enchantment such as candle magic, evocation, runes or offerings are all valid methods of reality manipulation. Use your intuition and experience as the best guide for how to influence events in line with your vision. More details on various techniques of reality manipulation are available in *Ovayki: Energized Info-Neurological Magic* (Vitimus, 2007).

The Demons Attached to Money

In modern and not so modern times, money has been greatly demonized. I am sure everyone has heard of "the man". Money is linked to "evil" collectively. Having too much or an abundance of money is considered evil by poorer people. Christianity and Islam both go so far as to make poverty a virtue.

Along with Christianity, Ceremonial magic also places a high priority on "spiritual" development as opposed to material gain. Lon DuQuette offers a story about his life as it was falling apart (2004). His teacher at that time strongly recommended not employing *the Goetia* because it would distract from building himself up spiritually. This negative attitude toward material success is reflected in Wicca, where it is not proper to charge for teachings or services in some cases. A strong dichotomy in Western thought emphasizes spiritual development, which is viewed as incompatible with material gain. This dichotomy is often deeply ingrained in all magicians coming from North America (perhaps less so in Europe).

On the flip side of things, many readers of this article probably come from a lower to middle class range of income. Having had the experience of poverty, including desperately needing money to buy food, I can say it isn't a pleasant experience. Everyone outside of the very rich probably has wanted material things (or needed material things), and not had the resources to get their needs met. The more basic the needed material things are, the less pleasant the feeling of need is. Needing food is not pleasant nor is not having the money for rent. Experiences create a world view that "money is scarce" and that world view is constantly reinforced by other people, corporations, and institutions. It shouldn't be a surprise that for many of us, money is scarce given the messages we receive.

The feeling of need is linked to products and manipulated by corporations to generate greater profits. We all have artificially conditioned desires and wants that through the clever use of advertising feel like "needs". Often, these needs are far greater then the available resources and corporations are quite adept at conditioning reward states to product and service purchase.

The unpleasantness of need, the deep conditioning that money is scarce, and the deeply ingrained idea that "money is evil" creates a psychological catch-22. The intended result is that people will either do nothing to better their situation or choose to pursue money as the primary goal. Fortunately, many products and services are offered to us to provide the momentary distraction we need to ignore this internal dissonance. This combination of conditioning creates a nice prison of control and it's a starting point for the self transformation that must occur before any wealth can be obtained.

As mentioned, money does things in a similar way that air and water does. Electricity powers this computer. Money allows us to survive in our current world. Outside of the cultural, parental, and institutional conditioning around it, money really was intended as a means of the transfer of goods and services. At one point, money would move from one person to another while each person was pursuing their own vision. This can be the model pursued again. The amount of money a person has relates to their ability to purchase goods and services around, but for many people the ability to move goods around becomes more important then actually moving the goods around. If you have lots of money, and no enjoyment of that money, is this wealth? In practical terms, the catch-22 of the money prison needs to be destroyed.

Evoking the Money Demons for a Long Needed Overhaul

Before we conjure up any personalized demons of money, we have to figure out what demons we have. My personal demons (issues) with money may not be the same as yours. Given current cultural pressures, some of the issues probably will be similar. First and foremost, relax and meditate for a while. Clear your mind until you get into a relaxed state. When you are in that relaxed state, write down any experiences you remember, beliefs, or feelings that come up when you think about money. Spend some time, while relaxed, just writing about your experiences with money.

A financially well-endowed person might have radically different issues with money then I might (in fact I can imagine that having excessive money would present the problem of motivation and figuring out what you actually want). The list you create will be completely your own, but while looking at the experiences and beliefs you have, distill the list down into categories of experience. Dig as deep as you can.

For me, I might boil my list down to:
Scarcity/Need
Feel good when I can buy stuff I want.
Selling out

Each negative category gives us clues to our internalized money demons. I can not possibly account for every personalized demon all the readers might have, but the scarcity or desperation demon is a good example to start with. Donald Michael Kraig offers a technique named Identify-Objectify-Banish as a method for making changes to our own internal make up (1988). Destroying internal demons as Kraig suggests is often difficult to do, but getting them to work for us is often a more useful trick (Dukes 2005). Let's go back to our original brainstorming and copy over all of the experiences that relate to money as scarce or where there was desperation over money. Relax again, clear your mind, and study the list.

Now, if you have been doing magical operations for a while, figure out the name and form of your own personal desperation money demon by your preferred method. One method I use is to formally banish, state my intent to find this particular personalized demon of money, and relax my mind. I will place a candle in front of a black scrying mirror while chanting in random speech and focusing deeply on the scrying mirror until I see a form in the mirror. As you are doing this, go back in your memory to the experiences you have had where money and desperation were combined (in the spirit model of thinking, these are instances where the demon manifested in your life). Continue remembering the different experiences you wrote down, while randomly chanting and while focusing on the mirror. When I use this technique, I tend to get stuck on a phrase. That is the name of the entity. If I see a form or spirit-like presence in the mirror, I will write out a description on paper. Sometimes, I will see a glyph representation which will act as a sigil link to the entity. Once I have the name of the entity, I will chant the name specifically and try to see what the entity looks like. If I have a sigil, I will concentrate on the sigil until I can see what the entity looks like. For verification, always use some sort of divination to check the sigil/name and appearance of an entity you scry in this manner.

Once you have the name and sigil for the particular attached/personal demon of money we can pull this demon into a formal ritual. If you have done the steps up to now, we can use the look and form of the creation for an evocation. There are countless ways to perform operations that will achieve the desired result, such as a ritual, hypnotic script, NLP technique, energy work, etc. I will present a simplified evocation for this particular attachment that has worked for me. For more information on evocation techniques (in line with the example below), see my book Ovayki: Energized Info-Neurological Magic.

Banish and state your intent to summon your personal "desperation" money demon that has a name and a sigil now. Draw an equilateral triangle on the floor with chalk in front of you. Surround the edges of the triangles with 3 words of power related to abundance. I might use the words abundance, wealth, and fortune, but the words should be strongly positive words that are in opposition to what issue you are calling forth. Place the sigil and name of the entity in the triangle. Go into a relaxed state of mind and let go of any tension. With all five of your physical senses, visualize and imagine a sphere of blue fire around you. If you have not done this sort of psychic shielding before, take a few minutes before the ritual and write down all the details of what a blue sphere of fire around you would feel like, look like, and even smell like. It is your blue sphere, so it need not have any excessive warmth in the flame. Keep relaxing until you feel like you are in a deep trance state.

Think about the joy and satisfaction that abundance, wealth, and fortune would bring you. With all of your 5 senses, keep imagining the joy, satisfaction, and happiness that having successfully completed your wealth vision would bring. Imagine those sensations, rising from the tips of your toes to the top of your head. See the completed vision, feeling how good it feels. Imagine those sensations arching like lighting from your hands into the walls of the triangle as you point toward the edges of the triangle. As you do these, imagine the triangle vibrating, glowing, and pulsing a bright blue. Try to use as many of your senses as you can. Once the triangle is empowered, chant the name of your personal money desperation demon while staring at its sigil that you placed in the triangle. Continue to chant and stare at the sigil while imagining the attached entity manifesting in the triangle (it may be helpful to have some incense or smoke rising from the triangle as a visual aid). If you do not have a sigil, simply start to imagine the form of your entity in the triangle. Try to use as many of your senses as you can in the ritual and go deeper into relaxation and trance. Roughly, this is a basic formula for evocation (without the god names and such).

Once you feel, see and know that the entity is present, start a dialog with the entity. Acknowledge the positive aspects of desperation and the motivation it provides. Usually any concept you are calling out like an entity is a well ingrained and conditioned idea. Keep telling it that you accept all the positive attributes it has, and that you are willing to listen to what it has to say. This step is a needed step before any dialog can occur (Dukes, 2005). At first, it may be hostile toward you. Stay calm, relaxed, and re-assert that you accept its positive attributes. This is a part of yourself, but you must stay in control of the situation. If you feel yourself slipping into a desperate state, you must go back to the feeling of abundance and joy. If you have trouble with the ritual, imagine yourself as that 50ft magician again and the entity as a tiny, tiny ant. Often, with many internal issues, merely evoking this part of yourself in this manner and accepting that this is part of you, does seem to help with the issue. At this point, there are an endless number of techniques that you can use to make the needed changes (which is just changing part of yourself).

One technique I use is to allow the sensation of abundance, wealth, and fortune to fill your thinking while you have your personal money demon in front of you. Visualize, feel, and even smell the imagined states of mind flowing out of your hands and into the triangle like a mist (it may be helpful to assign a color to the abundance state of mind and use that as part of the visualized mist). See your money demon surrounded by the mist, and as the mist surrounds the entity, see its form shift towards something you find more appealing. Converse with the entity and see how its attitude starts to shift. This is a type of energy manipulation and alchemy. It may take a few rituals to fully alchemize the issues that the creation represents, but you should be able to shift and heal the negative aspects of the part of yourself, while still allowing the positive aspects of this entity to help you on your quest. After the demon has been transmuted, call it up and use it to help you using the positive aspects that the entity has.

This technique can be used with any issue associated with money. The messages in our society are mostly negative regarding money. I find this exercise to be a useful tool and it is often a more empowering self process then hypnosis or NLP by itself (you are changing yourself, as opposed to an operator doing it for you).

Accepting the part, and accepting the positive aspects the part, can start a dialog. If a constructed form won't work with you, then use all of your senses and imagine binding it to a piece of paper and then destroy the paper. For dramatic effect, I will imagine binding the entity behind a mirror and then destroying and discarding the shards of the mirror (the idea being that the entity is trapped in the world behind the mirror). If you do destroy some part of yourself by a binding process, do make sure to replace it with a different way of thinking. Nature hates a void, even on the inside.

The Problem of Instant Gratification/ Inertia and Similarity

One of the greatest problems with money is the chain of conditioning occurring with our mass media, consumerist society. We are taught to buy things. It is ok to have things, but the key is to know what you want, versus what you are told to want. Many people will buy things to fulfill emotional needs. This is a carefully crafted illusion linking a positive emotional state to the purchase (but not ownership of a product). The conditioned emotional response occurs at the purchase time. We feel good because we are rewarding ourselves with stuff but the stuff is not stuff we really want or in line with our own vision. It serves as a temporary distraction.

Movies like the *The Secret* and the "abundance" movement maintain that if something feels good, you should do it. The problem with this stream of thinking is that many things such as buying things feel good but have very little long-term benefit. In many ways, the need to get temporary emotional boosts is detrimental to manifesting long-term wealth because people will often leverage their own finances into debt to get that emotional fix. Feeling good is conditioned with the purchase impulse. Feelings are completely within our own control regardless of the advertising that says otherwise. We can feel good by choosing to feel good whenever we want to. In practical terms, that is why we started the article with the laughter. If you still want something, after doing banishing and cleansing work, by all means go after it, but the linkage of emotional happiness to the purchase impulse as opposed to ownership/use is another clever demon (one I am not sure is redeemable). Try to relax and meditate on the idea. Does buying certain things produce an emotional reaction and if you have an emotional reaction to purchasing something why is the reaction present? How does your emotional state change the reaction you have to a purchase? Owning things is not at all a bad thing; being addicted to the purchase impulse, however, is counterproductive.

Creating the Money Angel of Yourself

Given the negative pressures associated money, it is important that we start to recondition the role of money. It is extremely difficult to possess large quantities of a substance you hate. One technique that I have seen in multiple books, articles and web pages is simply to repeat "I love money, and money loves me". Write down some memories and examples of what ecstatic joy feels like. Spend some time meditating on examples of what you consider pure joy after writing down what those words mean. From those memories, relax and relive the memories for a bit (and thus reproduce the feeling of joy). Now that you can remember what joy feels like, imagine what joy feels like directly. With this, we are well armed to start making ourselves a money attractor.

Start off with the laughter meditation for 15 minutes or so. After you have laughed for a bit of time, go back to your notes on what joy really feels like. As you are doing this, simply keep repeating "I love money and money loves me." Keep doing this for 30 minutes or so. Now, advanced experimenters should feel free to combine these techniques with visualizations of money coming towards them. I will use the microcosmic orbit while repeating "I love money and money loves me", imagining myself as a huge money electro-magnet (while cycling the energy around my body and feeling the joy course through my whole body).

If you can take on the state of joy, I personally have found that most money spells will work more effectively whether or not they are a simple candle spell or an evocation. Using this state in line with the big picture, however, has always given me the most happiness in the long run.

Vision Again, Honesty, Information and Obsession

No amount of mental conditioning, energy work, or magic can really help you if you make no progress towards conditions that you enjoy. That's the real secret of wealth generation. When work is expended into an area that is enjoyable to the magician, it no longer seems like work and doesn't drain the participant. Quite to the contrary, when you are doing something you love, you can work 12 hours a day and not be tired.

At some points in your plan, you will have to research and get more information. I can cast magic after magic to become a successful author, but learning about marketing is probably a skill that should be in my plan. In going over your plan, keep in account that you may have to research, study and learn skills to manifest that vision. This is only another way we all have to be honest with ourselves. The beautiful thing is that with the Internet and libraries, it is possible to learn those skills with hard work and little or no financial investment in many cases.

In pursuing a vision of wealth like this, there will always be bumps in the road. It is usually a good idea not to share your plan with all of your friends, associates, or family. Often, those closest to you will be the most critiquing and their criticism the most damaging. Take the constructive criticism and use it, but laugh at the malevolent criticism. There will be bumps in the road; laugh at those bumps. It is too easy to become obsessed over one roadblock in the process, but this is just another form of desperation. Wealth is about enjoyment and, in some ways, play.

Following your vision will take sacrifice and time. Being honest with yourself on what will make you happy is again paramount. Remember, there are most certainly financially successful examples of any thing you might love to do. Initially, I had mentioned that you should start with one vision, but that condition is an initial limitation to help start getting momentum towards building wealth. Of course, it is possible to pursue multiple avenues of obtaining wealth, once you are convinced that you can. Convincing yourself that you can, however, is easier when you have one focus to see real results. Take one step at a time, and the next thing you know you will have the wealth you desire. The great thing is that we can all have the wealth state we desire, so it will be my pleasure to see you there.

Bibliography

Alman, Brian M, Ph.D., and Lambrou, Peter, Ph.D. (1992). *Self-hypnosis: The complete manual for health and self-change (2nd Ed.).* New York: Brunner-Routledge.

Andreas, Steve, and Faulkner, Charles (Eds). (1994). *NLP: The new technology of achievement.* New York: HarperCollins Publishers Inc.

Byrne, Rhonda. (Producer), & Pachard, Henri (Director). (2006). *The Secret.* Australia: Prime Time Productions.

Carroll, Peter. "Chaos magic in Business". 2006. *Maybe Logic.* June 2006. <http://www.maybelogic.org/>

Carroll, Peter J. (1987). *Liber Null & Psychonaut: An Introduction to Chaos Magic.* York Beach, Maine: Samuel Weiser, Inc.

DuQuette, Lon Milo, and Hyatt, Christopher S., Ph.D. (2004). *Aleister Crowley's Illustrated goetia: Sexual evocation (3rd Ed.).* Tempe, Arizona: New Falcon Publications.

Dukes, Ramsey. (2005). *Uncle Ramsey's little book of demons.* London: Aeon Books Ltd.

Goodheart, Annette, Ph.D. (1994). *Laughter therapy: How to laugh about everything in your life that isn't really funny.* Santa Barbara, California: Less Stress Press.

Hine, Phil. (1999). *Condensed chaos: An introduction to chaos magic (3rd Ed.).* Tempe, Arizona: New Falcon Publications.

Jefferies, Ross. (1997). *How To Have Unstoppable Confidence and Power With Women.* [CD]. Published by Author.

Kraig, Donald. (1988). *Modern Magick: Eleven Lessons in the High Magickal Arts.* St. Paul, Minnesota. Llewellyn.

Lee, David. (2000). *The Wealth Magic Workbook or Buddy, Can you spare a paradigm?* London: Attractor Press.

Vitimus, Andrieh. (2007). *Ovayki: Energized Info-Neurological Magic.* Unpublished Manuscript (book available from the author).

Andrieh Vitimus has been a practicing magician for over 12 years in multiple systems. He has taught metaphysical classes at Alchemy Arts in Chicago for the last 5 years. He has had several store appearances through out the Midwest and has taught at conventions including Aeonfest, Ancient Ways, Real Witches Ball, Convocation, and Sirius Rising. Andrieh Vitimus's magical career, however, began with an undergraduate degree in psychology with a strong emphasis on cognitive science. He is a Usui and Karuna Reiki Master Teacher, and is working toward becoming a licensed hypnotherapist. In addition to the formal training as a Reiki master and Qigong practitioner, Andrieh Vitimus comes from a line of magically inclined individuals whose lineage include Asowge level Haitian Voodoo priests, Jesuit priests, psychics, and natural healers. He is a member of the prestigious Illuminatos of Thanateros, which is one of the most difficult magical organizations to enter. He can be reached via his website at http://www.andriehvitimus.com.

Strategic Magick
By Psyche

Wealth & Magick

It's ironic that in a field of study where numerous books advertise "prosperity spells" as get-rich-quick schemes, "serious" magicians often profess *never* to use magick to increase their wealth, advance their mundane careers, or otherwise directly enhance their material position. Oh sure, we can be rich in friends, optimistic thoughts, and find abundant, teeming wildlife a joy to behold, and yet there seems to be a lingering, but deeply ingrained belief that seeking money itself is not a reasonable magickal goal. Yet, without it, one cannot get very far in this world.

The modern separation of religion and state often seems to infuse magickal thought with the separation of the magickal or spiritual life from one's 'every day' life, or 'natural state'; with magick being reserved for closed temple doors, hidden beneath flowing robes in dark rooms thick with incense and the flicker of candlelight – or, at the very least, these are considered the ideal conditions for which magickal work *ought* to occur. This leaves many by the sidelines "waiting" for the correct set of circumstances to present themselves, the right tools to be acquired, or to satisfy some other set of conditions for which excuses are made to avoid achieving what you *really* want.

Aleister Crowley's classification of magick as the science and art of causing change to occur in conformity with will is almost universally known in magickal circles, and it's understood that this relates to all things mundane and spiritual: opening a door can be a magickal act when performed with conscious deliberation, and indeed, even such a simple practice can lead to encouraging results. He also frequently cited his Oath of the Abyss, to interpret every phenomenon as a particular dealing of God with his soul – a bold and deeply dedicated oath. Yet, some magicians today do not share this understanding, that the totality of one's experience in this world (and, for that matter, others) *can* be magickal.

Strategic Planning & SMART Goals

I work in finance, where my performance is measured by a balanced scorecard, which is a comprehensive overview of the goals I'm expected to achieve each fiscal year, broken down into various weighted components. The scorecard is then reviewed each quarter to evaluate how well each target is being met, make note where corrections are required, or set higher standards where targets have already been met or exceeded. This performance measurement framework is fairly common in the business world, so the strategic planning which underlies the goals may be familiar to many as well.

With some slight adaptation, this model can easily be adapted and effectively applied to magickal goal-setting as well. I've found it especially useful in results magick workings, and very well suited to wealth magick in particular. To explore this further, we'll use a recent example of a strategic statement of intent I used to boost my Tarot business, Psyche Tarot.

Wealth magick often has specific needs which need to be met, be it acquiring rent, money to travel, the elimination of a debt, or simply enough cash in pocket to buy another drink. These are all fine aims; however they are each very small in scope, and do not extend beyond the present or immediate future, and are vague in many respects. With strategic planning and the creation of SMART goals we may have a more clearly defined path, and therefore a better chance of succeeding in our aims: SMART goals are Specific, Measurable, Achievable, Realistic, and Time-bound – everything one needs to do well.

Wealth means having the resources available to pursue avenues of genuine interest. To attain an affluent state one needs to understand one's needs and desires, as well as examine the process required to manifest the desired result.

Identify a Goal

Most of us probably have at least a vague idea of something we'd like to accomplish at some point in our lives; perhaps you'd like to buy a house, learn Enochian, or simply provide a continuous stream of funds for that book addiction.

Ensure that your goal is something feasible; deciding to become an astronaut at seventy-six isn't very likely – with the education and health requirements for the job, the possibility is far too remote (sorry, grandpa).

Indeed, you may have a long list of things you'd like to get done; write everything down you can think of, from the small (buy a new CD) to the grand (become a maestro) to the exceptionally ambitious (headlining a world tour). Writing down your goals is an key step, it can allow you to view them more objectively; they're no longer idle thoughts, but a concrete list of things you'd like to accomplish in your lifetime, and this can be an important exercise in understanding your own drives and motivations – you may surprise yourself in discovering themes or desires you weren't previously aware of.

From this list, select *one* as something you're going to actively work on, something that gives you a sense of urgency with the weight of its importance. If it's not something you're *really* interested in, if it's not something that *truly* drives your desires, it's not likely something you'll invest a lot of time and energy into.

You can always return to the others at a later date, revisit and revise the list. Go over it in a year's time, five year's time, and see how it holds up: what you've already accomplished, and how important those things are you at that time.

Create a Vision

Now that you've considered your goal from all angles, it's time to create a mission statement which sums up everything you'd like to achieve in a few sentences. This needn't been an expression of your True Will, or Life's Purpose, but it should hold significance and encompass a message which inspires you to stick to it.

Keep it where you'll see it: on your bathroom mirror, your computer desktop, or your cubical – or wherever it will make the most impact to you, better still if it's in a place that directly reminds you of what it is you want to achieve. Make it a part of your daily mantra, if you swing that way.

Skill & Resource Assessment

Assess your skills and resources and determine what you're going to need to complete your goal. For example, if you want to go to university, consider what you'd like to study, where you'd like to go, how much tuition will cost, where you'll live, and so on.

Identify areas where you fall short and where difficulties may arise; consider how you might avoid them or handle them when possible. Where gaps are identified, consider potential solutions; if they support your main goal, even better.

It's important to realistically evaluate your goal and the likelihood if it being met. Start small to begin with; global domination may sound grand, but there are many smaller schemes which need to be pulled off before this can come to realization.

Roadblocks & Opportunities for Quick Wins

You've identified a goal, summed it up in a mission statement, identified possible problems, and begun to look for ways to overcome them. Plan for results – there's nothing strategic about crossing your arms behind your head, kicking back and idly wishing they come to pass.

Identifying and overcoming early roadblocks can provide opportunities for quick wins. In our university example, you may want to sigilize for student loan approvals, or begin taking the prerequisite classes, or perhaps perform some charismatic magick when approaching the admission offices. Completing each of these gets you closer to your goal, and provides encouraging feedback early in the process.

Employing Strategic Goals in Magick

I've been studying and reading Tarot for nearly fifteen years – reading at fundraisers, and lecturing at festivals, and for the past few years I've wanted to consolidate what I've learned into a book on the esoteric Tarot. I've written and rewritten outlines for the book, for the chapters, and even pieced odd bits together, but mostly I've procrastinated. Rushing seemed unnecessary, there was no hurry for me to actually dedicate a significant chunk of my time to completing it. Eventually, I realized that if I wanted to get serious about this, I'd have to formulate some sort of plan.

I already had years of experience working with Tarot, I'd read and accumulated more than a hundred books on Tarot, and more than forty decks. I had written articles and reviews for several magazines, and maintained several websites over the past eleven years. I seemed to be all set. I sat down and got to it, and, naturally, found that there were many additional books and decks that would add more depth to the work, and that it would be great if I could get feedback on what I'd written so far.

I already had it in the back of my mind that I wanted to expand the Tarot business I run on the side; it had been lagging recently. I wanted to bring in new clients and expand the services I was offering at the time. I had a rough idea about what I wanted to do, but lacked a concrete direction. To begin, I set about defining my goal:

Earn more money from Tarot.

Very basic, but also very vague. It wasn't *specific* (doing what with Tarot?) or *measurable* (how much money?), though it was *achievable* and *realistic*, if ambiguous, and it certainly wasn't *time-bound* (when would this money be in my pocket?). I needed to be more straightforward about what I was going to do and what results I was looking for, in short, I needed a clearer vision.

I thought about new ways I might make money from Tarot, and decided that I would teach two classes on the subject. I had a decent network of people I knew in the Pagan and occult communities, and I could be certain that at least a few people would be interested. I considered how much I could realistically expect, then reworked it, and came up with the following statement of intent:

It is my will to earn a minimum of $100 through teaching Tarot by July 1st, 2007.

Much better: it was *specific* (earn money from teaching Tarot), it was *measurable* (I had to earn $100), it was *achievable* ($100 isn't a lot of money), it was *realistic* (if I charged $20 a class I only needed five students), and *time-bound* (I had to accomplish this by as set date: July 1st, 2007). I allowed for the possibility of earning more, while setting a specific minimum target. It was clear, concise, and fit the requirements for a SMART goal: this was definitely something I could work with.

These classes would provide money for additional resources, and the students would provide feedback with questions and comments through the lectures: two birds, one stone.

With a clear mission in mind, I wrote the classes, created a flyer, and began advertising around the city to parties I knew would be interested, as well as tapping into my existing network of past clients. I decided I'd also create a sigil from the statement of intent to attract people to the classes.

I took the statement, removed the duplicate letters and numbers:

ITSMYWLOEARNUF$10HGCBJ27

and came up with a simplified symbolic reinterpretation of these characters:

The image was uncomplicated, easy to remember and visualize. I anthropomorphized it to have eyes to seek potential attendees, a mouth to speak to them, and a curled tail with which to draw them in.

I charged the sigil, and impressed it upon the flyers I was handing out, the e-mails being sent, and kept it in my mind's eye when I made calls to people I thought would be interested.

A week before the first class, I came to the realization that I'd achieved my goal: I had exactly a hundred dollars worth of students signed up; however, this left me only a few people attending each class. Indeed, $100 was easily achievable, but would make for two *very* small classes – something I'd neglected to take into account in my attempt to be conservative.

I only had a week, but I realized I needed to revise my original statement to attract greater numbers through increasing the desired amount:

> *It is my will to earn a minimum of* ***$200*** *through teaching Tarot by July 1st, 2007.*

Consequently, I revised my sigil slightly:

The tail now incorporated a '2' into its design.

I re-sent e-mails to those who had not yet responded, made follow up calls, and eventually found myself with two classes with a happy amount of people – indeed, more than the minimum amount set in my goal. The classes were successful, and I exceeded the result I had set out to accomplish: a magickal success.

When doing magick to support your goal, be sure you keep in mind what the purpose of each working is, and how it supports your ultimate aims. The reason I wanted the money described above wasn't merely to have more cash in hand, and had it been, teaching Tarot certainly was not the only or even the most direct route to achieve that. Rather, the money and the method feed into the work I'm doing in writing a book on Tarot – a single student's fee would not have been able to provide that. The statement I worked with, "to earn a minimum of $200 through teaching Tarot by July 1st, 2007" supports larger schemes. The money funds more material research (new books, decks, and so forth), and in giving these Tarot lectures I'm able to receive feedback for the work I've compiled and completed thus far.

Your workings should support the work you're doing. If they don't, you're diverting energy which could be put towards your main project.

Going Further

We've looked at the steps involved in setting a single strategic goal, but what about grander ambitions?

At work, my scorecard isn't a stand alone; its results roll up into my manager's, which rolls up into the vice president, and continues to roll up the chain ultimately to correspond to the vision and direction of the company as a whole – each person a brick in the pyramid that is The Company, and each partially responsible for achieving its ultimate aims. Magickal goals can often be similarly structured.

For greater targets one may wish to set an overall mission statement defining how a particular working will further that aim, or have at least have a more general aim in mind. However, note that the more specific you can be, the more likely you are to achieve results. If I had kept the first version of the goal, I could have made money with a single student, and the operation might still be considered a success, but $20 wouldn't be sufficient to keep me going in the direction I'm headed.

Completing and publishing my book on Tarot rolls up into a greater goal which I'll not speak of here, but you can see that each step supports the next step: earning money from Tarot lectures → funding

129

+ feedback → completing a book. Each small goal is a practical and *strategic* support for furthering my endeavors. Teaching paid classes has proved successful, and I'm likely to repeat it for further sections of my book.

Record Keeping

Keeping a journal or record is absolutely essential to any serious magickal practice. The style and content may vary, but one needs a record to refer back to note where progress has been made, especially for long term workings.

Using the Strategic Magick model for the actual creation of balanced scorecards to regularly measure and evaluate performance may seem anal retentive to even the most ceremonial of magicians. We need not go this far, simply keeping a clear understanding of the desired aims and the workings done to support these goals. The record can aid in maintaining consistent recognition of one's vision and path to success.

I use unlined 5 x 8¼" Moleskines, but any notebook will do. My preference is to maintain a hard copy rather than rely on computers, which aren't as easy to stuff in a knapsack for mountain retreats, never mind battery issues. Consider well the choice of lined versus unlined. Lined may facilitate clearer writing and if that's a concern, by all means use lined; but unlined better allows for illustrations (sigils, images that arise during ritual or contemplation, etc.).

The record can be written in code, in a mystical language or whichever script is deemed fit, as long as it's easily read by you at a later date.

Tracking one's progress – successes *and* failures – is one of the main benefits of keeping a magickal record. To this purpose, I write only on the right-hand side of the page, leaving the left blank until such time as I revisit what's been recorded.

Rather than a 'quarterly review', ensure that you set time apart each week, month, or year (as your practice deems necessary) to review what you've accomplished in the time passed. Note where corrections should be made, where you could improve, and don't be afraid to congratulate yourself where you've met with success. Date all entries and notes so when you revisit them again, you'll have an idea of where you were at.

Conclusion

Wealth is a means to an end, particularly when relating to money matters. For my Tarot lectures, it was a means to acquire additional materials and feedback for my research, while for another it may fund further educational and career pursuits. Rarely do we want money merely in and of itself, unless, perhaps, one wishes to recreate scenes from *Ducktales*, diving into a swimming pool filled with money like Scrooge McDuck (though it would seem rather dirty, uncomfortable and thus inadvisable, best of luck to you if that's your aim).

Forget generic prosperity spells and money potions, the truth is, the manifestation process is rarely easy. Rather, it tends to require a deep understanding and commitment to self to sustain and see it through to the end. Strategic Magick seeks to fix the will on a specific goal and *achieve it*.

Nico Mara-McKay (Psyche) lives and works in Toronto, Canada. By day Nico works for a major Canadian bank and by night writes freelance for various online and print publications, while maintaining the occult resource SpiralNature.com, and running a Tarot consultation business, PsycheTarot.com. Nico has been studying and practicing an eclectic assortment of occult disciplines for more than a decade.

Lakshmi Magick
By Hermeticusnath (Aion)

> *"1. O Mahamaya, abode of fortune,*
> *who art worshipped by the Devas, I*
> *salute Thee; O Mahalakshmi, wielder*
> *of conch, disc and mace, obeisance to Thee.*
> *2. My salutations to Thee, who art rider of*
> *the Garuda -thou art a terror to Asura*
> *Kola; O Devi Mahalakshmi, remover*
> *of all miseries, my obeisance to Thee.*
> *3. O Devi Mahalakshmi, who knowest*
> *all, giver of all boons, a terror to all*
> *the wicked, remover of all sorrow,*
> *obeisance to Thee.*
> *4. O Devi, giver of intelligence and*
> *success and of worldly enjoyment and*
> *liberation, Thou hast always the*
> *mystic symbols as Thy form, O*
> *Mahalakshmi, obeisance to Thee. "*
>
> *- Mahalakshmi Astakam Stotrum*[18]

Having been involved in a wide variety of Magicks for the last three decades (from Wicca to Tantra, Thelema, Vodou, Tibetan Buddhism, etc.), I have come to the inescapable conclusion that there are essentially two kinds of active magickal work.

The first is purely centered on the Self. It presupposes that magick is the art of changing reality through your own energy, will and focus without external help. Simple me = universe spell work, root work, sigil work and so on are all examples of this individualistic mode of imprinting one's will upon the universe. All diagrams, chants, and postures are seen as ways to raise "energized enthusiasm" in the individual to cause external change.

---

[18] Mahalakshmi Astakam Stotrum
http://sanskrit.safire.com/pdf/LAKSHMI.PDF

The other mode of magickal work involves calling upon a larger, greater or more extensive power-source than what is usually perceived as one's self. Thus calling upon a spirit, god/dess, demon, totem, savior or 'higher being' and petitioning or cajoling (or threatening) that supernatural ally into helping you cause changes in reality, whatever that may be.

In other words, from my experience, when you are seeking wealth through magick you have two basic techniques to choose from in terms of attaining the material items or riches you need.

You can do it by yourself, maybe create a charm or do a knot-work spell or draw a sigil based on I WANT MONEY! In this way you can do magick by generating your own energy through various means (exercise, mental focus, sex or whatever) and so imprint reality with your Will to receive wealth. Keeping always in mind the inherent ability of the universe to balance itself (sometimes rudely), one may offer some sort of sacrifice to unleash said energy.

Or in line with the second method mentioned above, you can get a "greater" being to do it for you by petitioning them. In other words, you can call upon a God, spirit, demon, one of the "mighty dead" or any other supernatural being that has powers you do not. Then, through devotion or cajoling (or demanding), get that the wealth you need.

As a bedrock Taoist, I'm perfectly aware that both of these modes are essentially the same in essence, that the gods, spirits, ancestors, tables, cars, jobs, etc. surrounding us are merely manifestations of mind and are illusionary, but in that case, the 'wealth' we are seeking is equally illusionary, so...

The point is this. If you and enjoy and live within the real world, the realm of illusion, and if you are seeking wealth then you have to play the game. Ah, but how will you magickally get the wealth you require? Are you going to do it yourself or get a god to do the work?

Both modes of working are viable. In general, if I have a specific wealth goal (paying off a student loan, for example) I will rely on my own magick and do a sigil or specific 'spell' that utilizes my personal power, but if I am looking for general wealth or for the universe to shift in such a way that a big-ticket item will appear at the right time & place (and all magick *is* timing) then I will let a god/dess do it for me.

My chosen paradigm is pantheism and for the last several decades my core pantheistic sect has been that of the Hindu Tantrik deities. Yet I never worked with the Goddess Lakshmi until my very smart wife discovered her and brought her into our ritual life, and with her came a whole flood of material prosperity!

Lakshmi has got to be the sweetest Goddess who ever existed, with an egregore bigger than Los Angeles and millions upon millions of fervent devotees who pour energy and love into her every day. That is quite a pond of prana to use, and once you take a swim in her bliss, you'll feel better for it.

Lakshmi is also one of the oldest deities on the planet. Crude carven images of her have been found that are over 6000 years old. One of her most primal images is as a lotus-headed and reclining naked goddess displaying her yoni for veneration. There is evidence that she was a primal Earth Mother long before inhabiting the formal Hindu Pantheon. Her creation myth is very telling. When the asuras (demons) and the gods were fighting over reality at the beginning of all things, they had a huge tug-of-war with the world serpent. The vast ocean of Samsara (reality) was churned and out of the whirlpool arose Lakshmi, and all the gods AND demons bowed to her and worshiped her as the manifested world. Here is a short description of her:

"The word 'Lakshmi' is derived from the Sanskrit word *Laksya*, meaning 'aim' or 'goal', and she is the goddess of wealth and prosperity, both material and spiritual[19]."

And from the same source, a clear description of her:

Lakshmi is depicted as a beautiful woman of golden complexion, with four hands, sitting or standing on a full-bloomed lotus and holding a lotus bud, which stands for beauty, purity and fertility. Her four hands represent the four ends of human life: dharma or righteousness, kama or desires, artha or wealth, and moksha or liberation from the cycle of birth and death. Cascades of gold coins are seen flowing from her hands, suggesting that those who worship her gain wealth. She always wears gold embroidered red clothes. Red symbolizes activity and the golden lining indicates prosperity[20].

Here is the kicker for eclectic ritualists like myself and, I would guess since you are reading this, like you: Lakshmi is accessible to EVERYONE. What I mean is that many gods, take Tara for an example, are supposedly only truly available as energy-streams to those

---

[19] About.com: Lakshmi, Goddess of Wealth & Beauty
http://hinduism.about.com/library/weekly/aa100900a.htm
[20] About.com: Lakshmi, Goddess of Wealth & Beauty
http://hinduism.about.com/library/weekly/aa100900a.htm

who have received special initiations or "tunings" to that specific wavelength. Anyone, the theory goes, can pray to Tara, but only those who have taken a Tara initiation can really gain the full effects of her blessings. Many religions, cults, sects and so on follow and profit from this idea, that if you have not been 'attuned' that you cannot reap benefits.

Whether these "initiatory gateways" are in fact doors to the real power of these spiritual aggregates is certainly up for discussion, but with Lakshmi it doesn't matter! Even in orthodox Hinduism (which does not much care for Tantrika) some gods are open for ALL and will bless anyone who wants it. Lakshmi is one of those big-hearted goddesses who is mother to all and will drop gold coins on anyone who is devout if they are polite and ask nicely.

Before going any further, let me clearly lay out the key Lakshmi information you will need to invoke her:

Some Lakshmi Correspondences for Magickal Works

Names: Lakshmi, Lakshmi Ma, Maha Lakshmi, Devi, Shri, Gauri, Ma, Shakti

Colors: Primarily red, also white, gold and green

Incense: Sandalwood

Offerings: Fruit, flowers, sweets, milk, ghee, yogurt & honey, money, kumkum paste or powder (sandalwood)

Mantras: The Seed Syllable is *shrim* (pronounced with a '*ng*' ending). A key Mantra is ***Om hrim shrim lakshmi namah svaha!***
There are many others, do some research!

Animal Vehicle: The owl, although elephants are often seen with her and she is very often displayed with Ganesh in places of business and home shrines.

Invocations: **The Mahalakshmi Astakam Stotrum** is among the most-used invocations of her. There are many possible versions, several are online and some of the best ones are referenced below. There are stotras, tantras and any number of devotional hymns to Lakshmi available. Again, a simple search online will reveal a treasure trove. Use what 'feels' right.

Symbol: The Shri Yantra

Holy Day: Friday is Lakshmi's day. In the year, Lakshmi has several key holy days, but the biggest is Diwali:

> **Diwali is also known as Deepawali, or the Festival of Lights. Light is significant in Hinduism because it signifies goodness. So, during the Festival of Lights, 'deeps', or oil lamps, are burned throughout the day and into the night to ward off darkness and evil. Homes are filled with these oil lamps, candles and lights. Diwali is celebrated on the last day of the last month of lunar calendar*."**[21]
>
> *(*Around late October, early November- it changes yearly.)*

Key Personal Information: Lakshmi is the wife (or goddess form of) Vishnu the preserver, but she is also called the 'wife of Rudra' (a wild form of Shiva) in the Lakshmiastakam Stotrum, which is one of her key magickal invocations. This tells us that Lakshmi is older and more primal than the Vedic gods, that she is firmly rooted in Pre-Dravidian mythos and is a manifestation of the Primal ancient Goddess called Shri or Devi or Shakti. Her symbol is the Shri Yantra, but this is also the yantra of Tripurasundhari (Shakti) so now we are realizing that they are all one & the same goddess, the Primal Mother whose primary color is red, Prakriti, the universal cosmic energy that pervades and manifests all things.

So, how did this lovely goddess change our lives and bring us much-needed wealth? Here come the testimonials!

Twenty years ago, when my wife and I first fell in love with Lakshmi, and it was really her doing, we instantly knew that Lakshmi was a way for two poor freaks to get some material wealth to have a better life. I was in more of a Shaivite mode, but my wife had other ideas and wanted us to create a nice home together. So we offered a little devotion (and some serious rituals) to Lakshmi and almost immediately it got us a small lovely rental house where we wanted to be. Of course, it was red. From then on we always had a Lakshmi shrine.

---

[21] Diwali Festival http://www.matiyapatidar.com/diwali_fest.htm

Years later, ready for a big shift, Lakshmi took us abroad to Japan and manifested a primo apartment in Tokyo overlooking Shinjuku and Mt Fuji. It was, of course, red brick.

And when we returned four years and one child later, we really needed a home and so we did a huge sigil and Lakshmi IXth degree Lammas ritual, first listing everything we wanted in a home on the sigil paper before offering it. And lo and behold! for a very low price a home manifested for us, in the woods but near the city. It had everything we'd asked for. And, yes, it is her color, very red.

Last year I did *puja* (ritual) to Lakshmi because I really needed a new used car and was having no luck finding a good one I could afford. I called on Lakshmi, Boom! Found it, just waiting for me. Not only is it red (I wanted blue) but now a Lakshmi sticker rides the back bumper.

I know when I'm onto a good thing. I truly love Lakshmi Ma, she is a kinder, gentler Babalon for those of you who work with that goddess.

Here are the steps to wealth and fame, or they could be if she blesses you:

Basic Procedure for Lakshmi Work

1 First, decide on whether you want to have a long-term relationship with this goddess. Read about her, get to know her and find out more about her personality, history, likes and dislikes and so on. Read her myths and find a version of the Mahalakshmi Astakam Stotrum. It is a powerful key ritual (and some web sites with this invocation are listed at the end). If you decide you want to work with her and have a *bhakti* (devotional) relationship, then find a nice image (*murti*) of her as well as a small image of the shri yantra. Look in import stores or even download one from a web site.

2 Set up a small shrine to her. It could be shared space or separate place. In stores they are near the cash register, in homes they are usually near the doorway or where finances are dealt with! Banish it as you like, clean it well, and offer something to the elephant-headed god Ganesh (his mantra is *Om Gam Ganipataye Namah!*) to clear away all obstacles.

3 Then, in a ritual of your own devising, on a full moon, set up the image of Lakshmi in the shrine. Place the shri yantra

before her. Set up the things she likes about her framed image or statue (see the correspondences above) and chant her mantra 108x. You should then read a hymn to her. It can be one that you have created or found or a version of the Lakshmiastakam Stotrum (again, see sites below.) "Open the eyes" of the Lakshmi image by anointing them with sacred oil or another substance. Now she is present. Ring a bell to awaken her. With an open heart offer to Lakshmi sweets, incense, candles, milk or yogurt (and wine if you are a heathen tantrik!) and flowers, all that she might like. Conch shells, jars of coins, coconuts are all sacred to her. I often give her candy bars, be creative! Honor her as mom from the heart. Call to her and she will come.

4 Place a flower in the center of the shri yantra, she will manifest here.

5 When she is present, ask for what you want, the more intensely the better, Mother always wants to help! Do this while focusing on the flower on the shri yantra and on her image. Ring a bell, invoke with passion! Try sex magick if you like or dance, do yoga, do art, or sing: all are marvelous offerings to Devi and if she is pleased, and she is an easy one to please, then she gives and gives and gives.

6 After the active ritual and asking, silently meditate and commune with her. See yourself receiving the wealth you are asking for as a shower of gold flowing from her hand. End the ritual appropriately, with gratitude. It is common to end by saying *Om Shanti Shiva Shakti* (Peace, the union of Shiva/Shakti). I always finally offer prosperity to everyone as well by chanting "health, wealth, prosperity and freedom to all beings!"! Ring the bell and banish as you like.

7 Afterwards: *Be generous!* As the mystic gold of Lakshmi in whatever forms falls upon you, remember that a healthy organism takes *and* gives, so make sure the wealth flows through you in your daily life and Lakshmi will be your friend. When you travel, spread the wealth to those in need, when going out, tip well and so on. Don't be cheap, circulate the wealth, and give to charities, *give!* The curse of wealth is greed! and it banishes Lakshmi and pisses her off. Giving money or sharing whatever gifts Lakshmi lays on you is also a crucial earthing of your working and a key offering to Lakshmi who is The World. I always give

money to homeless people after a Lakshmi working: do what is right for you.

8 Ongoing: Be grateful for what you get. *Always* thank Maha Lakshmi! Maintain your Lakshmi shrine or alter. Keep gifting her. Use other magicks and things with her, she is a great sport! My Shakti and I often honor her at the full moon. We find that we get gifts from her in this way even when we are not consciously asking for anything. Lakshmi can also be called upon to protect your home and hearth, for this is her domain.

9 What is the Downside to Lakshmi work? You gain easily weight, develop a desire for sweets, become a mellower and more giving person (a wimp if overdosing) and you might become a materialistic yuppie, but don't let that happen to you. She would not be pleased.

Well! I think that anyone with the wisdom to be reading this book can take it from here if they wish to court and dally with Shri Maha Lakshmi. I have found that she gives what is needed when it is. This is very mellow wealth magick with almost no negative blowback, but it comes with a price. Though she is virtually 100% beneficent, it is still a relationship and all relationships (as we know) take work, so treat her and her shrine with respect. Be kind, have fun, don't be greedy and you will get what you need!

May Lakshmi bless and empower you with the wealth you Will with Love!

Two examples of the *Mahalakshmi Astakam Stotrum*

-Mahalakshmi Astakam Stotrum
http://sanskrit.safire.com/pdf/LAKSHMI.PDF

-Mahalakshmi Astakam Stotrum
http://www.celextel.org/stotrasdevi/mahalakshmiashtakam.html

Aion *(Hermeticusnath)* aka Denny Sargent is the author of several books including *Global Ritualism, The Tao of Birthdays, Your Guardian Angel and You* and the newly published *Clean Sweep* (on Banishing). For more info: http://www.psychicsophia.com/aion

How I Used Wealth Magic to Move to Portland
By Taylor Ellwood

In February 2007, I realized with complete certainty that I wanted to move to Portland, OR. Lupa and I had just finished vending and presenting at the Magickal Winter Weekend festival. What struck me most about that weekend was how active and supportive the community was, and how much I wanted to belong to a community like that. As we drove home to Seattle, a place I didn't like and felt little comfort in I told Lupa how much I wanted to live in Portland and all the reasons why. At the time, she seemed to agree with me and I called some of my friends in Portland to tell them the good news.

A week later, Lupa brought up a point that had been bothering her all week long. She'd finally, recently gotten her first tech writing contract. If we were to move at the end of the lease, it would be in April, but her contract wouldn't end until November. She didn't want to break her contract early, and told me she wanted to stay in Seattle until it was done. To say I wasn't happy would be an exaggeration. I suddenly felt as if I'd been offered the world and then had it taken away. When I posted my dilemma to a trusted list of friends the best answer I got was to either tough it out or consider moving down to Portland without her. Neither choice was viable and I was frustrated. Yet within a couple of weeks, by happy coincidence, Lupa was informed by her boss that her contract was ending early because he couldn't find time to train her.

Never one to look askance at opportunity I pointed out to her that I felt that the loss of her job was a sign from the powers that be that Portland was the way to go. After some thought, Lupa agreed and we decided that we were Portland bound. The only question was how we were going to land what we needed, i.e. a job, a place to live, etc., in a manner that didn't hurt our finances. As I'd already been doing a lot of reading about finances and been working hard at changing my internal attitude to wealth I was fairly certain I could come up with some viable magic that could land us in Portland safe and sound.

The First Step: Building up Energy for the Move

I did face a minor problem with our move to Portland. At the end of May, Lupa and I were scheduled to present at an event in Virginia and our tickets had already been paid for by the hosting event. The flight was scheduled to leave from SeaTac. I knew I could probably reorganize the trip to fly from PDX, but I also knew it would cost money. What this meant was that I had to time everything just right so that I moved down to Portland at the end of May instead of the end of April, when our least was due to be up.

I contacted our landlord and got her to agree to a one month extension of our lease, if we needed it. Then I started job hunting. I put my resume up on all the main career boards and I started contacting recruiters for jobs. I also put a lot of energy work into the job hunt, using the Taoist technique of the macrocosmic circuit breath to accumulate energy and then direct that energy toward the job hunt. However, the energy work wasn't done to get a job right away. Instead it was driven toward making sure that everything fell properly into place exactly when we needed it and not one moment sooner. I didn't want a job in Portland until after our flight out of Seatac had been taken care of, so although I started job hunting at the beginning of March, I actually directed a lot of my magical efforts toward building the energy up and waiting for just the right moment to release that energy.

For many magicians, it seems that magic is results driven. Do some magic, get a result and move on with your life. I'm not really a results driven magician. I think results are important, but only in the sense that they confirm that your process is working or if it needs refining. To me, doing magic that requires a build-up and release is a process oriented approach. It doesn't focus on manifesting results right away and even when results manifest it doesn't stop with just those results. Instead the magician uses the results to build the process up, accumulating more and more energy, until eventually the energy can't be contained and it has to be released. The key is to release that energy in exactly the direction you want it to manifest.

The Second Step: Attracting Wealth and the Right Job

While doing the energy work, I also did several other magical workings that were designed to attract two important desires I wanted to manifest in Portland. The first important desire was to attract more wealth in my life. I reasoned that just by moving to Portland we could save money, but money alone wasn't what I wanted. Money is one external result or manifestation of wealth, but it doesn't comprise the entirety of what wealth can be.

To me the desire for wealth in Portland represented a variety of results I associated with being wealthy. Accumulating, saving, and using money wisely was one form of wealth I had already begun to manifest in my life, but wealth is more than just that. I still wanted to continue accumulating money, but I also wanted a less stressful commute, where I didn't have to drive nearly as much. I wanted to live in a really nice neighborhood, close to everything, but still have an affordable price on the actual housing. I also wanted to live close to the friends I knew, while having the opportunity to meet more people. I wanted to work magic with a group of people. Finally, I wanted to live in an area where I could continue to find and cultivate opportunities that would help me manifest one of my long term desires, which is to become independent from working a 9-5 job for someone else. All of these desires represented wealth to me and were fairly important in determining if Portland was the place to go.

The second important desire was to get a job at the right time. While it was true that I was already doing energy work, I also felt that having a little bit of help in finding a job couldn't hurt. I wanted to find the best possible opportunities so I could manifest them into my life.

I used two methods for working with these desires. The first method involved incorporating a statement of desire into my daily prayers. Each day I would pray to manifest the wealth of the universe into my life and also pray to manifest a job in Portland.

The second method involved creating two paintings. One painting represented wealth. I painted it to look like a magical dollar bill. I created the painting to act as a repository of wealth energy. The wealthier I got, the more wealth energy went to it, so that it could amplify that wealth energy into my life. The second painting was a painting used to create an entity that would help me find jobs. In the painting the entity stood above a jar with sigils. The jar with sigils stores away job hunting energy that the entity gathers. When I need that energy, I simply evoke the entity and have it release the job hunting energy. A nice extra feature is that even when I'm working at a job this entity can still gather energy from that job in anticipation of future job hunts.

As we'll see later, this step of the process had mixed results, which means that some of my approaches need to be refined further to really manifest the success I desired.

The Third Step: Undoing the Saboteur

Both Lupa and I have a tendency to sabotage ourselves just when it seems like we're getting what we really want. She has a tendency to worry a lot and thus project the worst possible outcome on a situation. My sabotaging when it comes to wealth is much more insidious, because it's rather subtle. The sabotage is a tendency to believe that success can only be gained with lots of struggle. I was told this a lot by my mother, probably because she did have to struggle a lot in her life, but also because she discourages success when she sees other people manifesting it. I didn't realize until very recently that I actually believed that I had to struggle before I could succeed. It was only in the process of manifesting a move to Portland that I actually came face to face with this sabotaging pattern of behavior.

About a month before we were going to move, I suddenly experienced an onset of doubt about moving to Portland. I began to convince myself that maybe it wasn't such a good idea, that maybe I should give Seattle another chance (even though I knew that Seattle doesn't fit me). I realized I doubted myself, but I pegged it for potential moving jitters, even as I half-seriously considered just moving to a new place in Seattle and continuing to live there. Fortunately I was smart enough to realize that I needed to get a relatively objective opinion.

As it happened, at the end of April, Lupa and I were being flown out to Oberlin College to present workshops and my friend Maryam told me she'd be able to see me that day. Since she didn't live in Seattle or Portland she had no vested interest in whether I stayed in one place or moved to another. I asked her if she would be willing to do a reading for me, and she graciously agreed. During this trip, I was also reading a book, *Secrets of the Millionaire Mind* by T. Harv Eker and between the Tarot reading and that book I came to fully realize how I was sabotaging myself by giving into the doubt I felt.

Maryam and I both do a style of Tarot reading which I would call freestyle reading. Instead of using set spreads for reading the cards, we randomly develop a spread for each situation. By doing this we avoid letting ourselves confuse the meaning of the cards with the meaning of the spread. Both she and I have noted that traditional spreads have associated meanings with the way the cards are set up, which can consequently confuse the actual reading. I shuffled the cards and created a V spread with a triangle in the middle of it. One branch of the V represented my choice to live in Seattle, and the other branch represented Portland.

The cards for Seattle had a lot of heat and fire imagery. The end result of them also indicated that I would have to put a universe's worth of effort into creating what I wanted. Any success I might find would involve dealing with lots of obstacles. Intriguingly enough, while doing this reading, I overheard one person ask where Taylor was and another mention that Taylor was sick (We were in a university building with students). There was a great amount of coincidence in that, which I consider a sign of the divine rapping me over the head to make sure I understood that Seattle never was, nor would be my home.

The cards for Portland had lots of water imagery and suggestions of refreshment and relaxation. They represented the path of least resistance toward the results I wanted. The cards also suggested that I would be delving even deeper into the internal journeys I was on. The result card was the woman of crystals, which has been a card I'd been using to represent myself in some of my magical workings. The overall card suggested synergy, that in each case an alignment of purpose and energy would manifest, but one approach would be much better than another.

The reading helped me realize that I had an important choice to make, and that choice wasn't so much about where I lived (though that was important too!), so much as it was about whether I wanted to continue living a life where I expected to overcome obstacles to achieve success, or whether I wanted to live a life where I took the path of least resistance and effort to achieve the greatest impact.

As I mentioned above, I was reading Eker's book at the time. Between the Tarot reading and his book I realized something very important. Some of the exercises in his book showed me how my attitudes toward finances were symptomatic of the attitude I had toward living life. I had always asked myself if I could handle failure, but in reading his book I realized that living life isn't about handling failure. People handle and live with failure everyday. Failure is easy to live with. Each day people fail and yet each day people pick themselves up, dust off, and get back to living, or at least surviving.

So if I already lived with failure, what was the question I really had to ask? At first, I thought it was, "Can I handle success?" But I realized I already knew the answer to that question. I could, can and will always be able to risk being successful, because I've already been successful. This didn't mean I couldn't learn to handle greater degrees of success. We can all learn to handle greater degrees of success and I agree with Eker that people internally decide their own capacity for handling success. But the real question, the true secret to wealth of any kind, was I could risk being happy?

I have to admit that until fairly recently I've not lived a very happy life. I spent most of my twenties struggling toward happiness, keyword being struggled. So when I asked myself if I could risk being happy, my first reaction was, "No." I meditated on that answer, wanting to know why I felt this way. My meditation revealed that I had come expect that in order to be happy or be successful I had to struggle in life. I didn't like having that behavior pattern in me. I knew I needed to deconstruct it.

The Tarot reading I got from Maryam showed me how to deconstruct this behavior pattern. I could choose to continue living in Seattle and settle for a life of struggle in order to obtain success and happiness, or I could take the path of least resistance, and risk being happy without having to struggle. The choice was obvious. Any doubts I had about moving to Portland faded. I knew our move would be successful and that we would have jobs, a place to live, and a lot more happiness than we'd ever find in Seattle. And the land in Portland sung to me in a way that Seattle never had. So why ignore that call, why settle for less? I told Lupa the result of the Tarot reading and she agreed with me.

Step Four: Telling Lies to Make them into Reality

Once we'd decided to move to Portland, there was just one more problem to solve. I had to figure out how to quit my job. See, I really liked my job. In fact, it was the only thing I liked about Seattle. I worked with good people and I enjoyed the work I did, plus I had enough free time at work, occasionally to actually do my own work and my team lead didn't care as long as I kept producing the results he wanted. Not only that, but we'd finally gotten a second tech writer and he was thrilled to have two of us.

But my team lead did have one flaw in the sense that he took anyone leaving his group very personally and could make their lives hell for the last couple weeks. I love harmony and I didn't want to tell him I was leaving unless I could provide a really good reason for leaving. Telling him I was moving to Portland because Seattle didn't feel right to me just didn't seem like a reason that would work. I had to figure out a good reason to explain why we were moving. And I did.

I told him that my wife had gotten a full time job with a publishing company in Portland. It was a lie, but it worked...no politics, no drama, a very happy send off, and a bit of magic…because even though the words uttered were a lie at the time, I believed that words can shape reality and my belief was that my wife would get a job as an editor, if enough people believed what I told them. Belief is energy and if you can direct that energy you can manifest anything.

As another bit of word magic, I also wrote a couple articles and indicated that I would be living in Portland in May 2007. Set a belief in written word and you give it more impetus to spread…that was Burrough's approach to magic and one I've used to good effect. I figured if I set a definite date for when we'd live in Portland, it could only help the magic manifest what we needed.

Conclusion: The Process Manifests Results

As I mentioned above, both Lupa and I tend to worry. One of the principles in Eker's book was that people who had negative attitudes attracted negativity to them (2005). I'd seen this principle in both our lives a number of times. I'll admit that a big part of the problem with living in Seattle was my attitude. I attracted a lot of the negativity that I felt there (though not all of it…I do trust my intuition when it says this place doesn't want you here). I knew that even though we were both firm on living in Portland that we'd both need to help each other with the occasional bout of doubt and negativity that inevitably happens when you get ready to move and not everything is secure. I also knew that she and I had differing beliefs about security. She admitted she needed security. I could care less, because for me security was a delusion people tried to convince themselves was real. But I could respect her need for it, because I had needed it once as well, until the realities of graduate school stripped away the scales on my eyes.

We'd both done a lot of magic. After the trip to Oberlin was over, other than my daily prayers, I stopped doing the magic and let the process manifest the results (i.e. signs) we needed to have to know we were on the right track. And the results always came in at just the right time. Whenever either of us expressed doubt within a day something would happen that confirmed we were on the right path. For example, we started looking for a place to live, but we just couldn't seem to find a place in the area we wanted to live. We'd remarked half-jokingly that it would be really cool if the people that lived about some friends moved out. Lo and behold our friends told us that they were moving out and we began the process of securing the place we wanted to live in. When one of us expressed doubts about finding a job, an interview would be offered a day or so later.

Every time we needed confirmation, it came. Each result that manifested confirmed that the process was working. When we moved down to Portland everything pretty much fell into place. Some results indicated that the process needed to be refined, but overall I was pleased. We moved into the home we wanted, Lupa did get a job as an editor at a company, and I also landed a short term job. In fact, my job was the only fly in the ointment. While I'd gotten a job at the right time, it wasn't quite the job I had wanted. I had hoped for a shorter commute, health benefits, and much more stable work. Yet when I looked back on what I did, I realized I hadn't specified those needs in the prayers I'd recited or the related job magic. I had left the interpretation open to the magic and it gone down the route of least resistance, though not the best results. Instead of being discouraged I've already begun refining it for my next job hunt.

What we can learn from my mistake is that when magic doesn't work it's usually because of human error. By not being as specific as possible, I manifested what was easy to manifest, but not necessarily what was best. Still, overall the wealth magic was a success and both Lupa and I are living a very wealthy life indeed.

Bibliography

Eker, T. Harv. (2005). *Secrets of the millionaire mind: Mastering the inner game of wealth.* New York: HarperCollins Publishers, Inc.

The Wealth Magician's Allies
By Jozef Karika

Magical thinking differs from wakeful, linear, and grammatical thinking, not just in terms of imagination, but also in terms of personification. In the context of magical thinking, it's true that there are far fewer metaphors than an ordinary person would think. The roots of this approach extend back to animism. Metaphorical thinking, with elements of animism, may be implemented even today in our hectic and technologically advanced times.

Ramsey Dukes created his concept of cyber-animism by combining elements of magical thinking with modern-day cybernetics. When a certain level of complexity is achieved in any system or pattern, be it in the external or internal world, one may expect certain "independence" or − "self consciousness" in that system or pattern. With the help of special (i.e. magical) techniques, one can develop specific types of interaction between a sufficiently complex pattern and the magician. One example is a pattern of constantly repeated failure, a device that keeps breaking down, traffic lights showing red when you are in a hurry, etc. Although it sounds bizarre, Dukes hints at the fact, that in the first moment with technical breakdowns, despite the rational surface layer, we react as if we expected technology to interact with our impulses.

Of course we don't have to become shamans and develop communication with stones or trees, if we find it too strange. It is important to develop this ability and magical point of view just in those fields that can demonstrably benefit us. Moreover, such an approach often has a rational core.

According to Dukes − and the recent researches published in the magazine *Current Anthropology* − the current branch of humans has won the primeval evolutionary struggle because it behaved far more socially than the members of other branches. This was the case with the original primates, as well as with the latter Neanderthals and the species *Homo sapiens*. Even though the Neanderthals closely knew the life and habits of their game, and trapped it in the sophisticated mechanical traps, these skills weren't essential for survival in the evolutionary struggle because they lived in small, isolated groups. *Homo sapiens*, on the other hand, had migrated through vast places and constantly developed their social contacts. It was precisely this skill that enabled them to survive in the harsh times of need.

Dukes develops the idea and comes to the conclusion that man as a social being uses his brain potential to the fullest when he approaches his environment socially instead of mechanistically. Of course, the mechanistic approach has its importance which should not be underestimated (e.g. to a large extent it forms the basis of scientific thinking). However, the social approach to one's environment – that is, when we behave as if our environment was a living entity – sometimes offers a necessary and different point of view, often leading to a surprising – and rational – solution.

Dukes illustrates this with a simple example of a car that "doesn't want" to start when we are in a hurry. From the usual and sober viewpoint, the search for any connections between your current situation and the car's unwillingness to cooperate is inadmissible, even ridiculous. However, if just for a moment we admit that the car perceives us (and we wonder "How does it know?"), we begin to treat the car as a living being, which may lead not only to the solution, but also to other interesting thoughts. For example, we start to think about just how can the car know when we are in a hurry? Then we proceed to thoroughly analyze our behavior under these conditions, and realize that when we hurry, we tend to shut the car's door with a greater force than usually, which in turn interferes with the important connection in the ignition system. An irrational (magical) approach thus disclosed the rational core of the problem.

This example is simple and meant purely for illustration. It only shows that the possibilities for utilizing other than usual worldviews really exist, and they can really work. What's important is which approach offers you more options when solving real life problems. How much of this principle can be utilized in money magic? Quite a lot. In the cyber-animistic concept, financial products and markets are seen as independent entities, as beings or spirits.

Power of the Allies

Magicians have always used allies, spirits that were of service in many ways, multiplying their power, which can work miracles. Such allies of the wealth magician are financial products, stock markets, commodity, or foreign exchange markets. These are not the only allies; There are, of course, others, but we will use the above mentioned ones as an example to illustrate some aspects of their practical magical use.

Let's go back to the power of spirits. In money magic, the equivalent of such power is what the commodity or exchange markets can offer – namely an extremely high leverage. For example when dealing with gold on the commodity market, you can control a 100 troy ounce contract worth 43,000 USD[22] for weeks or months, after blocking the sum of 2,000 USD on your account (the so called "margin"). If the price of gold increases 1 dollar per troy ounce (which is a very small change when it comes to gold), the trader earns 100 USD, because he is really in control of a 100 troy ounce contract. When doing business on forex (an international monetary market) you can utilize leverage up to 400:1, which practically means that after you lay down a 2.500 USD deposit (margin), you are enabled to do business with the amount of 1.000.000 USD. Sounds unbelievable, right? The power of these allies is really unbelievable.

You alone can't achieve such leverage. To gain it, it's necessary to enter into an alliance with the spirit of the market and go with the flow. As is the case with any other powerful spirit, when you interact with these spirits, the success of your venture depends on you and your will, intelligence, knowledge, and self-discipline, whether these extreme powers lift you to the top, or smash you to the ground and rob you of everything you have.

For example, the spirits of commodity markets are extremely powerful entities, some even on the level of deities. They know no mercy, and they work in a quite simple manner. Like vampires, they absorb the "blood" (life energy and time, contained in the invested money of traders) of some 80 % of the involved traders and transfer it to the other 20% of them. Using the commodity market spirits is basically a form of energy vampirism of money magic, because the immense profit of the small part of traders is generated merely by the loss of 80% of other traders. Nothing is created, you only use your skills to gain the favor of the spirit of the market, or to get a close knowledge of the spirit and be able to foresee his moves, and thus secure the flow of others' money to your account.

I could write a lot about the ethical side of this way of earning a fortune. It's certainly not for everyone, since it requires certain shark-like qualities, e.g. some amount of disregard and cruelty. You must not care whether you have taken away some trader's last money, even if he is in the middle of a serious life crisis, or if he has afterwards committed suicide and left behind three children with no provision. If

---

[22] At the time of writing.

you want to be a successful trader, you just can't think this way[23]. You simply step into the game, in which you can gain or lose, and you fight for your own wealth according to the jungle law. Others do the same thing. Everybody knows the risks. Business is not a game for sensitive people. It is a battleground.

Nature of the Spirit of the Market

The leverage rate that the spirit of the market, bank product, or investment opportunity can offer to you is at the same time indicator of the extent to which it can cause damage to you, how fast you can lose your money and even become fatally indebted[24]. The leverage rate is the indicator of the ferocity or peacefulness of these spirits. For example when "investing" your money in most bank products, the leverage rate is low, sometimes pitiably low, and it might not even exceed the annual inflation rate. On the other hand, when depositing your money to a certificate bank account, the risk of losing your money (e.g. bankruptcy of the bank) is similarly low, and your promised profit is practically guaranteed. The risk of losing your home, in this case, – which can theoretically happen when behaving recklessly on the commodity market – equals zero. Investing in the stock markets or in real estate is an entirely different case.

It's important to learn to distinguish the basic traits of ferocity or peacefulness of the spirits. You do this by observing markets, investment products and opportunities through the magical point of view. Create your own hierarchy of spirits according to their ferocity, from the wildest ones, capable of bringing quick money, to the slowest – most careful ones, the spirits that move slowly, but sure and without unpleasant surprises. Choose those spirits whose "character traits" most closely match yours, and who best resemble your ideas about the

---

[23] The failure of many traders on the markets is, apart from other reasons, caused by insufficient acceptance of the ethical side of this type of business. This important point is often downplayed and ignored, but it is still active in one's subconscious. The potential trader on the commodity markets should deal with this aspect and other negative subconscious programs. One should consider if he really wants to make money this way. If his confidence is wavering he should use the techniques of banishing and illumination.

[24] On the commodity markets, for example, your profit or loss from a single trade can theoretically be limitless. If you don't use the stop loss, your loss can amount not just to the amount of invested sum, it can reach a hundredth, or even a thousandth multiple of all your possession's worth.

character of business. If you are more of a slow, prudent disposition, don't choose spirits that require the highest speed and extremely strong nerve. On the contrary, if you are a quick, lively person, focus on the spirits excelling in speed. However, be aware not to overestimate your powers. In such case your uncontrolled inner speed "adds" to the momentum of the market, and you may lose your money twice as fast. If your quickness manifests in a rather negative way, choose a slower market where you can train the control of your "recklessness". Only after you learn some self-control can you increase your speed.

After you have defined the hierarchy of ferocity, you can progress to focus your magical vision. Even in every field of business there are several sub-groups differing in character. For example when it comes to common investment funds offered by some banks, you can come across some highly risky stock investment funds, in which you can lose half of your savings plus a considerable fee charged by the asset management company regardless of how your investment is doing[25]. On the contrary, while some commodity markets are considered very ferocious and wild (e.g. oil), others are quite peaceful and suitable for beginners (e.g. corn, soybeans or frozen orange juice). If you want to know the personality of the particular market's spirit,

---

[25] For this reason I don't consider common funds to be very effective investment tool. Not only you have practically no control of your invested money but on top of that you pay initial fee (sometimes leaving fee too), depository fee and managerial fee. All regardless of how effectively your money is invested. Revenues are not guaranteed unless you invest into a secured fund that guarantees you certain, usually low profit, over several years. Even then, you cannot access your money if you want to get the profit, but over the years you have to pay various fees. There comes the unavoidable thought that the fund administrators can make 1000 % p.a. when trading your money on commodity markets or stock exchanges, maybe even more, but you get paid maybe 3 to 5 % p.a. after deducting the fees. That is, if you are lucky - since negative results are legal, too. This wouldn't come as a surprise after several cases of investment fund money frauds.

However, if you have enough time and other worries than managing your money and if you don't aspire to high revenues, you don't have to avoid common funds. Under certain circumstances this can be one of the wisest forms of investing your money. It is always better to earn 5 % p.a. over five years than to lose all your money in two months speculating on the commodity markets. To keep your money is sometimes a more important ability than to earn great amounts.

look for its volatility. Volatility is the indicator of the market's liveliness and momentum. You can make more money in less time in lively markets, but you can also lose it very quickly, if you don't act in time. Other helpful indicators of the spirit's character are its liquidity and volume (meaning the volume of money traded in a given period of time).

When analyzing the character of a particular market's spirit you shouldn't forget the market's trend charts at least in three time intervals, e.g. daily, weekly, and monthly. A price trend chart of a particular market is the record of the traders' group reactions, i.e. a graphic record of mass psychology. Technical analysis of such charts knows tens, even hundreds of various patterns repeatedly occurring in the charts. From these patterns, one can predict the future trends on the market to some extent of probability (since human mass reactions tend to reoccur). When thoroughly analyzing any market, you can perceive some recurring patterns. These are the actual graphic record of the market's spirit influencing the participating traders. The pattern is a graphic sigil of the spirit, discovered from the mass acting under its influence.

After grasping the character of the market's spirit and perceiving some of its characteristic qualities, you can create symbols of this spirit (e.g. a sigil), that are readily recognized by your subconscious, and use them in practical magic. (Apart from creating a graphic sigil, you can include the spirit's picture – e.g. according to the market's commodity, size the symbol according to volatility, create the spirit's name after the particular market's name etc., your creativity should not be limited). Invocations of the spirit of the particular market can be of service, in order to unite with it and learn its movements. In the same way you can include the spirit's symbol in the simple binding rituals to minimize the hypnotizing influence that the markets usually exert on the investors. The elementary prerequisite for successful trading is discipline and the precise follow-up of your business plan, which is quite difficult to keep if you are under the influence of the spirit of the market.

Usage of a living symbol of the market (gained from your own insight) for divination appears to be suitable only if you can make a sufficiently precise predetermination of the time period you are going to focus divination on. If you trade intraday, say, with a 5 minute chart, you will have difficulties in divination because there is no chance to gain necessary distance from the object of divination. On the other hand, if you focus your divination on several weeks in advance (in case of long term, positional trading) many factors can step into the game and meddle with the expected result. Even if you do know what the future movements of the market will be, it won't help you much, not even in case of a successful divination. Long term experience will show you that you can suffer greatest loss even at times, when the movements of the market seem to be good for you. It is the paradox of trading, in which self-discipline and following your business plan matter more than predicting the movements of the market. Divination can therefore be used as a helpful complementary means, but not as a basis of your work.

Apart from the spirit hierarchy, learn to perceive the aspect of time. Every market has its own ascending cycle (the bull trend) and descending cycle (the bear trend). When dealing with the money magic entities, these cycles are equivalents of astrological or tattvic cycles of the traditional magician working with elemental or planetary entities. If you closely observe and learn to feel the moods of the market, you will realize that there are periods of time when it is best not to invest.

You will also notice that various *moods* of the market, as they are usually called in business circles, do not always depend on the moods prevalent among the participating investors or traders. Dukes shows us the example of the so-called "nervous market" that occurs often when the majority of investors are not nervous, as we would expect, but on the contrary when they are passive. Thus he demonstrates the presence of a phenomenon, where a complex system can create its own structures, which cannot be directly derived from the mechanically added structures of the system's individual elements.

One important observation to conclude: when attempting to personify the market avoid the elementary mistake of transferring the personified, relationship-based approach to the trading itself. You can approach the market via a relationship, personify it in order to "merge" with it or to work magically with its living symbols, but as soon as you actually start trading, your approach must be perfectly mechanistic and impersonal. You can only be friends with the dragon if you are not sitting on his back and riding him. As soon as you step into the game, the control and rules must replace everything personal and relationship-based. If you transfer the personal approach to the field requiring mechanic approach and discipline, you will lose your money. When asked what the typical mistake of trading beginners is, Bruce Kovner, one of the greatest stock market legends and market wizards said: "They personalize the market. A common mistake is to think of the market as a personal nemesis. The market, of course, is totally impersonal; it doesn't care whether you make money or not. Whenever a trader says, 'I wish,' or 'I hope,' he is engaging in a destructive way of thinking because it takes attention away from the diagnostic process." ([2], 82).

The Most Important Ally

Your first, central, and most important ally in the sphere of money magic is your bank. It is an ally that under certain conditions can provide you priceless service; it can support you, protect you and effectively help in hard times. It is not an ally with a wild character, and if you choose wisely, it will become an important stabilizing element in your money magic practice.

At the same time it is an extremely powerful ally. The extent to which you can use its power is directly dependent on your financial discipline, and grows proportionally to the development of this ability. If your financial discipline is strong, you can gain the support of this great power. On the contrary, if your discipline is weak, this ally can lead you to financial disaster, because it knows no compromise and it is very consistent when it comes to signed contracts. It doesn't matter if it works for you or against you.

Apart from the support it can provide, this ally is also important as a teacher, because it will only lend you as much power as it expects you to be able to handle – based on the records of your previous financial history. A bank can be only rarely tricked. Even if you manage to trick them and gain more energy concentrated in money than they would give you based on their assessment, you will most probably suffer harm. It is the bank's interest to lead you to financial discipline and general stability. This is the foundation for a reciprocal symbiotic relationship.

There are, from the viewpoint of magic other financial institutions that can provide you with money – demonic allies. However, the pact with them is drafted in such a way, that it secretly expects your lack of financial discipline and general instability in life, and it exploits that to a much greater extent compared to the support provided to you. These allies are very dangerous – they are financial vampires that will mercilessly ruin your existence even for a small loan. Do not contact them at all, or at least contact them with utmost carefulness. Their characteristic traits are for example a very easy and informal process of entering the pact, as well as big investments to massive and alluring advertising campaigns. They often approach you at times of great financial crisis and promise you easy access to money. Be careful and always think twice, if they really try to help you, or if they want to get you into much greater problems through the lure of solving the small ones.

Many people feel uncomfortable when negotiating with bank managers. This feeling comes from the subconscious perception of the fact that talking to the bank manager is an illusion. You don't talk to a human being. Not in the magical sense. You are talking to an ally whose nature is not human. The bank manager's personality is just the mediator. The manager doesn't follow his own personal rules (even though he does put a part of his personality into the communication). He receives information from you, evaluates it, and compares to the bank's rules. The manager is a medium; he is in a sense possessed by the spirit of the bank during his working hours. The spirit can be seen as the body of the bank's internal policies. When you are negotiating with a bank manager, you are in fact talking through him to a deity, like in the ancient oracles.

This comparison is not exaggerated at all. In Phillips's book *Seven Laws of Money*, many recent studies compare the bank premises to the sacred places of the modern day. Psychological researches of people's behavior in bank premises confirm that entering the bank premises activates in most people a behavioral pattern similar to the patterns activated when believers enter their temples. A bank is a sanctuary, where dwells one of the most powerful gods of this age. Judging from the influence it is perhaps *the* most powerful one. For the biggest part of their visitors, the temples of many religions provide the mere spectacle of architecture. It's as if the spirit of their deity was not present anymore. Not so in the banks. Almost everybody feels the living presence of their god there. Learn to perceive the architecture of banks and to interpret it. Notice the location and the building of a particular bank. All of this is an expression of power for the spirit of the particular bank.

You don't necessarily have to choose the most powerful bank allies. Do a research of their individual attributes related to your personal needs. Banks are not uniform. Their spirits are diverse and therefore it is important to choose an ally that is in harmony with your own personal character and your financial objective.

After you have chosen a bank and opened your personal or business account you must act very responsibly. This account is your basic magical tool; it is your portal to the financial "astral plane", the world of financial spirits and currents. Every action connected with your account, be it great or small, is an act of money magic and leaves a trace. These traces are then evaluated and the ally treats you accordingly. It opens to you, or it turns away from you. Therefore it is important to view every operation on your account as an act of magic.

Never allow any frivolousness in this space. Don't overdraw your account more than once or twice a year. If you overdraw your account, pay your debt as soon as possible. The ally won't be angry with you if you overdraw more often. On the contrary, this kind of behavior generates its profit, but you will gradually lose its respect and become part of the grey mass of its providers of nourishment. The more often it happens, the more you will lose your power when contacting the ally. In the end it will turn you into a slave and bind you to itself. The ally is neither good nor bad. It is neutral. It only copies your behavior. If possible, try to make regular deposits. Keep the account balance as high, or as stable as you can. It pleases and calms the ally, because it is a reflection of your own stability, and you will keep its respect.

Plutonian Powers

Pluto was the dark Roman god of the underworld and…wealth. He was one of the most powerful antique gods. Even today we call the wealthy upper class "plutocracy". Pluto's reign extends to this day, even though its forms have changed. A great wealth is connected to the powers of underworld, in both meanings of the word. Balzac wrote *"Behind every great wealth there is a crime."*

One of the basic requirements for a magician is, if possible, not to be naïve. We must not think that great wealth exists without the cooperation, or at least tolerance or silent agreement with the Plutonian powers of the underworld. Dave Lee describes the Plutonian face of money as their dark spell or dark beauty and writes: "Under the surface of money, under its official faces, lies the hidden world of money. This is where money shades into political power (plutocracy and corruption), organized crime, insider trading and large-scale corporate fraud. The images associated with this aspect of money are highly glamorous, in the way that power is sexy." ([1], 22). Let us clear up any potential misunderstanding. I don't suggest you to enter pacts or alliance with the underworld. On the contrary, I recommend that your path to wealth should be as much as possible within the limits of law. However, when dealing in this field, even if you try hard you probably won't be able to avoid situations where you will need the help of Plutonian powers. It is better to count on that and be prepared.

Trying to get into contact with the Plutonian powers, or enter pacts with them when you *already have a problem* will place you in a very disadvantageous position. Pluto's earthly representatives are very intelligent in this respect, and will notice immediately if you contact them because *you are already in trouble.* In such cases they will require a greater sacrifice for their deity. And you will bring the sacrifice, because you will have no other option. Therefore be foreseeing and get into contact with them, however superficial and brief, before you come across real problems. Like the traditional magician that uses demonic powers for some purposes, the money magician has to contact his plutonian *allies* in some cases, for specific purposes.

This aspect of money magic is not pleasant, and it destroys many illusions. To enter the arena of business and financial activities without considering this point means not learning the lesson about the occasional need for roughness. Since the world is ruled by human greed, even with the best of intentions you probably won't be able to avoid situations where you will need the authority, or even the punishing hand of Plutonian powers.

I am not trying to say that you will never be able to manage your business without these types of allies. In fact it would be much better if you did manage it without them. But let's be realistic and count on them as alternatives, if they are needed. Can you afford the risk of dealing with such situations without the pact with Plutonian powers, who are the only ones capable of solving difficult problems effectively? You will have to find your own answer to this question.

To conclude, the best teachers of Plutonian rules, their living invocation, focus, and synchronicity triggers can be the pop-cultural forms from the novels by Mario Puzo, such as Vito or Don Michael Corleone, or any similar, sufficiently Plutonian archetypal character. Their visible expression in the sphere of wealth is a dark, often black and elegant appearance, with a somewhat reptilian air about them.

Important Rule

In this section we will introduce one of the most important rules of the approach to the *allies*. We will disclose the secret which has caused many existential tragedies and disasters. The greater the power and ferocity a spirit of a market, stock exchange, product etc. has (expressed in its high leverage), the more stable, consistent, and organized must be your life. The wildness of the ally, whose power you are about to use, has to be counterbalanced with proportionate stability in your life. Otherwise the power will destroy you.

People used to say that top traders and stock brokers are rather bleak, boring people. Of course this isn't always necessary true, but even if it's only sometimes true, it confirms the natural laws in the field. Every ally requires from his tamer certain mental qualities. In the same way, work with every ally shapes your psyche. If you want to work with the most powerful financial spirits, you have to pay the price of changing your inner world. You have to minimize impulsiveness, irregularity, spontaneity, and other qualities generally considered as funny. If you cannot control these qualities, the power of your allies will grind you to dust (especially when it comes to financial markets, stock exchanges and certain types of business). Of course, this self-control will over time become automatic and change you, though not always in a way you would wish for.

A similar principle can be applied in other fields, for example in the sphere of magic. Many people are surprised when they learn that the many representatives of chaos magic current lead rather conservative, apparently boring personal lives. Judging from their texts, one would expect a wild, extravagant, and spontaneous way of life. Nothing could be further from the truth. There are of course exceptions to the rule, but the chaos magicians exploring the extremely powerful parts of human psyche and playing with the most powerful magical forces would not be able to withstand the subversive effects of these forces if they weren't strongly rooted in their normal daily lives. Therefore, if you want to work with powerful financial spirits in a long term, do your best to stabilize, calm down and organize your life. This includes all spheres: relationships, family, work and the social sphere.

Bibliography

LEE, D. (2005). *The Wealth Magic Workbook*. Attractor, London.

SCHWAGER, J. D. (1993). *Market Wizards -- Interviews with Top Traders*. CollinsBusiness, New York.

Jozef Karika is the author of *Slavonic Magick*, *The Zones of Shadow*, and *Money Magic*. He has published articles in *Konton* magazine and *Chaos International*. He has two degrees, one in philosophy and one in history and works as historian and TV redactor in Slovakia. He has practiced magic for twelve years, starting first with Bardon's system, then Thelema, and in the last few years chaos magic.

Using Collage for Growing Wealth: Theory and Practice
By Wes Unruh[26]

I can tell you that I'm telling the truth, but I don't swear on anything because ultimately I'm just a sentence, made up of letters, that is being interpreted through a symbolic set you were forced to learn to get by in this society. You're reading this far, so you've made some concessions in your consciousness that allows communication with the not-you in general and with this printed matter specifically. That means you've learned to use a symbolic structure that didn't generate from within you. To learn magic that I'm talking about, specifically in the context of the rest of the time I have with you in this piece, you'll need to use a symbolic structure that you personally have generated for yourself. I know I'm asking a lot, and I'm just a few letters on paper. Still, I'm asking for your attention long enough so I can explain what I mean, so you'll be able to interpret my conclusions about using collage to grow wealth.

What I use is an internal symbolic set that I've produced through doodling and free association, and combine it with atavistic symbolic sets as I see fit. Here's the dirty version; I use magic to program my subconscious so it's always there pushing me in the direction I need to go to accomplish the statements of intent that I've set forth. The essence of magic is the setting of goals, but with a whole shitload of psychic oomph. I encode meaning. Or inter it, as encryption could be seen as entombing meaning, although I prefer to see it as the seeding of meaning. Seeds look nothing like the plant that bore them or the plant that they become. Creating directions for your subconscious mind is done by allowing the collusion of desire from the primal or sleeping self to generate private symbolic structures that 'just feel right' when you align them with a list of demands. Ask yourself to find the symbols, and they'll catch your eye. Create and recreate the symbol until it is immediate, until you can recall the construction of its form flawlessly, and you'll have created an associative link between the conscious self and the subconscious mind.

---

[26] Editor's Note: To see the Wealth Magic Collage for this article please go to: http://wu.sauceruney.com//WealthMagic/

Broken down to this level, there are a few things I know I'm jumping across here very quickly. The most important is that the subconscious mind will not work in collusion with the conscious self (you who are reading this are mostly being driven by the conscious self) if the conscious self does not learn to interpret the differences and the gradients of consciousness, all of which entail a totality of the self as opposed to conscious, subconscious, and unconscious as discrete elements. You're all of them things bound up in one. If you get all those parts on the same page, all working as one, if all your parts as a whole are focused, reality warps to accommodate your passage. So how do you get there?

To work towards wealth is to work towards growth, towards prosperity, and towards fecundity. And wealth is not by any means money. If you want to summon a spirit and force it to take you to buried gold, there's a book or two with those specific formulas out there, and they've got very detailed instructions. Not that I'm turning down gold, but what I'm saying is that in reality what you want when you say you want money is a limitless expense account that is, in turn, tax deductible. Time is not money; instead time and money together make a lifestyle. You've got to create a place for wealth in your life because otherwise your personal expectations are set so low that you will subconsciously sabotage any financial success you do have.

So this work of learning your own inner language is incredibly important. Here's the thing though, and this is where it gets fucked up... most everyone's subconscious landscape is already somewhat populated by the symbol systems around them. There are a few symbol systems so well thought-out and so deeply ingrained that they can be used *as* an internal symbolism, and I've got my own theories on why that works based on genetic memory. Take that as a plug for your favorite magical alphabet if you'd like, as I know some of you reading these words are probably well versed in Enochian, Theban, Runic, or kabbalistic scripting, but I still believe this learning of your own techniques of internal communication are fundamental in plotting a course through coincidence. Here's where it comes together-learning the language of the inner world, of the unconscious and subconscious mind, can only be approached indirectly.

There are a lot of reasons why this is, and because I'm skimming so roughly over a century of soft sciences and magical currents to get to this article I'm only going to give you one: your unconscious mind is that which you cannot be consciously aware of; it is those thoughts which you are incapable of thinking. Your subconscious reacts to the currents of your unconscious mind and intrudes on your linear thoughts to indicate an unconscious disturbance. Your subconscious does want to communicate with your conscious self, and so learning to communicate is actually pretty easy once you get things moving.

I know there are a few ways out there to create a language for yourself, private signs and symbols, new words that you use to then delineate full sentences, private paragraphs, which then can be essentialized into a solitary letter of an even greater word. Peter Carroll's "Alphabet of Desire" is as good an entry point as any, but what I personally did was come up with vast lists of symbols from throughout history, and study them. There's an excellent book out there called *Dictionary of Symbols* by Carl Liungman, and since publication it has grown into a website at Symbols.Com, which went a long way toward providing me access to a vast assortment of iconographic symbols to browse. Start here if you're going to go about collecting symbols and sigils from which to generate your own dialogs with your unconscious mind and the universe at large.

From this start I added runes into the mix, astrological and alchemical symbols, various sigils and seals I've used for whatever reason throughout childhood, and then seasoned it with hours and hours of active sigil creation ala A. O. Spare's nearly incoherent directions. This has done two things for me. First, and most importantly, I seem to be more or less entirely in tune with my unconscious motivations, which has the effect of improving the rapidity in which what I say I'm going to do and what I actually do occur. Secondly, it's given me a symbolic set to work from for sorcerous intentions. The fact that everyone's subconscious landscape has been littered with the symbolism of the monoculture in which we find ourselves means that internally we've already impressed some measure of meaning and value into these symbols, and as such the apprehending of value, the sort of dispelling of obfuscation, can be achieved by creating a massive catalog for oneself of all the symbols one feels even the vaguest tingling of resonance, and putting it up where they can all be examined.

For wealth magic I highly recommend bricolage, because of our material culture's obsession with the image, there's plenty of images out there that represent a concrete accretion of your chosen lifestyle that preparing enough source material can never be a problem. The act of collage, especially on a massive scale across different sensory channels, becomes a dance with your subconscious mind. Often I have found that forms I sense in a collage become a sigil I will sketch out, which then represents the intention stated at the onset of the collage, and in doing a collage of this magnitude you'll likely discover multiple layers of symbolic meaning as the collage comes together. So now that you've got the basic theory from which I work, let me take you through the exact process I used to get to this point in my own life.

When I began I only had the vaguest ideas of what kind of career and lifestyle I wanted. I generated a very specific set of instructions by following a series of questions and then answering these questions in as detailed a method as possible. This is the planning stage, and occurs on the conscious level. Here are the questions I answered in my notebook: What do I want to wear for work? What schedule do I want? What kind of physical activity? Do I want to work indoors or out? Do I want to work with people, animals, or technology? How much money yearly do I want to make? Do I want continuing education to be a part of my job? What temperature do I want my work environment to be? Where do I envision my job taking me geographically? What kind of audio do I want present in my environment? What responsibilities do I desire? What kind of personality do I want my boss to exhibit? What kind of recognition do I want? How is this recognition going to be expressed?

Taking each of these questions in turn and answering them as honestly as possible in sentence form, gave me not only a grasp on the kind of career I wanted, it also created a snapshot of the kind of lifestyle I wished to maintain. I then took a piece of paper and wrote out all of my answers around the edge of the paper in the smallest possible script, spiraling inward towards the center and pinned it in the center to my wall. For about three weeks every day when I woke up, I would spin the paper around, reading the lines, as a way of really re-ingesting my intentions. I was associating my conscious intentions with that piece of paper until I felt it had firmly established itself in my unconsciousness, at which point I took a sigil I'd developed that represented the personal growth possible with a steady income, and placed that in the center of this paper, then framed the entire thing.

This is the first stage of the process, and was a protracted programming of my unconsciousness with my conscious intentions. The next stage was to create a new sigil which represented wealth, and at the same time to create a collage with graphical representations of images I associated with that wealth. For myself, I see wealth as potential for life experience, and as security in the face of the unexpected. The sigil I created and anchored in my unconscious mind at this point needed to be something I couldn't lose, something I'd not ever be able to let go of, and as such I ended up using the lines in my left palm. Overlaying this sigil onto the digital collage creates a knot of meaning that is revitalized subconsciously every time I glance at my left hand, and that repetition reinforcing this focus helps maintain an ongoing relationship between my lifestyle and my career.

Creating the collage is a symbolic gesture as well, as it helps trigger a foundation for the social and interrelated aspects of wealth. I've been using digital collage of imagery for a few years as part of my magical practice, in part because I believe that the Internet is reflective of the spiritual or Akashic interconnectedness of the human race. When we work together to define our reality, when groups come together to accomplish a goal, there is an energy that arises from that group which helps sustain and drive the group to their goal. This has rapidly become understood in the business and entrepreneur community as masterminding, but the truth is even an individual can tap into this collective co-creational process through acts of collage.

Here's how I work with digital collage using search engines: I state I intend to create a collage, and for what purpose. I sit in front of the computer and think of a keyword that somehow implies or relates to this purpose; in this case I'd pull from my answers above, and put that keyword into an image search. The first result that catches my eye from that image search I then save to a folder, and I jump immediately to the next keyword, working as fast as possible to keep my conscious mind from interfering too much by decision-making. The conscious self has had its turn, with the question and answer session, and it's now the subconscious mind's task to find links between your unconscious and the great pool of collective behaviors which have seeded the Internet with images that align with the keywords you're tossing into the search engine. Let this happen as fast as possible - if you find yourself wandering off topic, getting distracted, or otherwise losing the thread, stop. Usually after an hour or so of this, I have a database of images which I then dump into an image program.

I like having a huge space to work on, and I move the images around until they're all more or less partially visible, partially obscure. I try to keep from consciously placing images next to each other. If I can get my conscious mind to more or less stick with keeping the images all on the same space, I can usually keep from being overly aware of what it is that I'm seeing. This sleight of mind stuff is discussed in sigil creation in enough places online that I don't feel I need to justify its importance -- suffice it to say it keeps the lust of result at bay so you can really bridge the internal desire with the external events that bring about wealth. You've got to accept that while you can know what you want, you can't control how it will manifest. Creating a collage in this fashion helps open you up to that interaction with the universe on a larger scale, and through lines of association that are already laid out by existing social networks. Using images culled from the net, I am tapping into the society from out of which the very notion of wealth arises.

Once the collage is finished, I placed my personal sigil of wealth into the collage several days later, so this collage now signifies both my own desires and the reflection of those desires against the symbolic structures that are accredited by the rest of society. This imagery should be placed in the same area as the other piece with the sigil representing the personal growth that the wealth would provide.

So, to sum up the process, I first started out by creating a sigil that represented the growth I'd have with a sustainable lifestyle. I then carefully and in great detail described that lifestyle, and then made an artifact that combined those answers with that first sigil. Then secondly I created a sigil that specifically signified wealth, then allowed my subconscious mind to select imagery from the net that related to keywords I associated with wealth, many of those keywords arising from the lifestyle narrative in part one, that also created connections with society at large. This last step is very important, because wealth can only be defined against a social backdrop.

This works, or rather, it has worked for me. But like I said at the beginning, I'm just a few letters, placed carefully on a page. Feel free to riff off of these ideas, or to construct your own narrative entirely. In any case, have fun.

-Wes Unruh, 8-07

Wes Unruh lives in upstate New York with his fiance, Shira and his familiar, Gargi. He's one of the founding editors of the fringe culture site Alterati.com, and has written extensively on the overlap of magic, memetics, and group minds for an up-coming book. He is also writing a novel in four parts that covers the shift from human to transhuman and the problematic nature of immortality. He's perhaps best known for the audio noise sculpture project Philip K Nixon, and was a panelist and speaker at Esozone 2007. More of his work is available via his website at WesUnruh.Com

The Use of Money in Magic
By Vincent Stevens, I.S.U.A.G.

Introduction:

The idea of using actual physical money in a magical activity is a subject that will produce diverse reactions. To some, it may seem quite logical, while to others it seems crude or primitive. I myself find using it in magical acts to be simply useful and practical. This essay explores four methods for using physical money in magical activities related to finance.

Sometimes the best magical tool may be in your wallet or your purse.

Why Use Real Money?

Physical cash, to put it simply, is a powerful tool. We've been used to it all of our lives, most likely, and it has powerful associations for us. Even if the medium of money, be it paper or otherwise unremarkable metals, has little hard value, our emotional and mental associations with it are strong. Thus, acting with and on actual money in magical practice is a simple and effective way to use those associations, mental states, and emotions.

Magic, after all, is about those connections and the energies they raise. Acting upon physical money works with those connections and associations. A dollar bill, a handful of coins, provide a quick, effective, and guaranteed way to rally subtle connections and thoughts you may not even be aware of.

Quite simply, you can't beat using the real thing. Even if money is symbolic - a bill or coin's value is usually symbolic, not due to direct exchange - the symbolism is very real.

With that being said, let's take a look at four ways to use hard currency in your financial magic, and the results I've had.

Technique I: Sacrifice

Sacrifice is an age-old technique in magic, religion, and related behavior - you essentially give something to whatever powers you're interacting with to ask for favors, honor them, make an economic exchange, or interact socially. Sacrifice, despite the unsavory connotations attributed to it in modern culture, comes from words meaning "to make sacred."

In today's age of electronic fund transfers and currency, the old sacrificial ideas of goats and knives, burnt offerings, and the like isn't really necessary (as well as being overly messy, cruel, expensive, and likely to get you into trouble with the SPCA). Today, money is far more important than livestock - and so if you must make a sacrifice, consider hard cash instead of warm blood. The goats will thank you.

If you're engaged in making a sacrifice, using money is an excellent way to do it. The emotional, symbolic, and practical power of money is very powerful magically, enough so that we often forget it. Again, we are so used to money's power, we don't recognize it.

So, if you've got a god or spirit to invoke, consider a sacrifice of money. It may not be as spectacular as the Old Days, but it's faster, more meaningful to you, and won't wake the neighbors. A few tips:

* A good sacrifice is, simply, to donate to an appropriate institution for the god or spirit in question. If the entity already has an established temple or organization you respect, donate there. If not, donate to something appropriate to the entity in question - if you're invoking Thoth, donate to a literacy fund, for instance.
* Use actual bills/coins if at all possible. The symbolic value of hard, physical cash should not be underestimated. It is probably more powerful for you, the magician, than simply filling out a PayPal voucher - though who knows how that may change in the next few decades.
* Try placing appropriate signs, symbols, seals, or sigils on the currency in question. This may not always be possible, but if it's an anonymous donation, it may be easier (and money gets enough marking on it no one may note it). This helps provide further connection to your act and focuses your intent.
* Any receipts or forms you receive may also be appropriate for ritual acts. You may also work them into talismans.
* Give enough to "feel" it. The act of sacrifice is nothing if there's no meaning to what you do. Give until it hurts" may be an overstatement, but it should be enough that it's meaningful. Meaning after all helps power magic.

My experience with sacrifice has been very positive. The act of getting a bill from an ATM, sigilizing it, giving it away, produces very powerful reactions, and can be ritualized easily. It also commits you to your intent - putting your money where your mouth is, as it were. Parting with that $50.00, as I did in my first experiment with using money in sacrifice, was a profound experience - I was parting with a large amount, giving it to a cause associated with my work, and it truly let me feel the connection to what I was doing.

Technique II: Sigilization by Spending

By now there are few people unfamiliar with the sigilization technique - turn a sentence into letters (by knocking out repeated letters), turn the remaining letters into a symbol, and then launch it by focusing on the symbol in some intense state and (traditionally) forgetting it. It's the Philips screwdriver of modern magic - a handy tool for many occasions that's reasonably precise. If on the off chance you haven't heard of sigilization and sigil magic, a half hour on the internet should clear up any ignorance.

Most variants in sigil magic that I see provide imaginative, or at least different ways, to launch the sigils. A technique I devised is to launch a sigil via that common (thus easy to forget), yet emotionally charged (if often forgotten) action of spending cash. The method is quite simple:

* Compose your statement of intent and create the sigil.
* Place the sigil on a bill. I find it especially effective (and fun) to try to work it into existing markings and symbols on the bill.
* You may also want to put additional seals, signs, and sigils on the bill as appropriate. Planetary sigils to invoke appropriate forces, for instance, could be placed elsewhere.
* Spend the bill as soon as you can. The usual action of forgetting a sigil is easy as you're so used to spending money anyway. Even popping the bill into a vending machine may be useful.

I have used this method for a number of financially-related situations - and only financial situations. I had results every time I used it - within a week. However, the results were unpredictable - some were shallow or partial. As I have only done this as a "quickie" spell, I plan to explore putting more of a focused ritual around this activity in the future and see if the results are more consistent.

As of this writing, I've only used this technique for financially related magic because of the financial associations of the act of spending. You may wish to explore non-financial goals on your own (I should note I don't think forgetting a sigil is always necessary, but that's for a different essay entirely.).

Technique III: Talismans

Building on Technique II, you can also work money into long-term talismans. Work bills or coins into the very construction your talismans and amulets. Working bills into talismans not only adds the symbolic association of money, but it is also, frankly, fun. It produces the mental and emotional involvement crucial to good magic, and opens you up to new ideas via figuring out new ways to craft things. A few suggestions:

* If you have paper talismans or other talismans made from flat surfaces, put bills between the surfaces.
* If you do a more "crafty" talisman, such as a prosperity bottle, incorporate the money into it directly.
* Constructing an actual talisman out of money can provide an interesting challenge, such as the famous Chinese coin blades.

Also consider the possibility of mixing talismanic techniques with the sigilization and/or sacrifice technique. If your talisman has a specific purpose, once that purpose is complete, take the bill(s) in question and spend them or sacrifice them as needed to seal/complete the magic. In the case of sacrifice, you'll want to use an appropriate amount of money as noted above. Otherwise, I find that the amount used doesn't seem to matter.

In my experiments, I've found this to be an effective way to produce results with financial talismans. Much like the work with sigilization, the results can be fast, if a bit erratic - producing results in an on again/off again manner. I have found it more effective and stable than the sigilization method as I have practiced it.

As a suggestion for the creatively-inclined, consider the possibility of using origami to turn a properly sigilized/marked bill into a talisman by folding it into an appropriate form.

Technique IV: Contact

Building on Technique II and III is an area I am experimenting of as of this writing: using sigils, money, and spending to contact entities involving finance. In my case, I'm trying to contact the "spirit" of money itself. The concept is relatively simple:

* Determine what you are trying to contact: the spirit of money, finance, or a particular deity associated with money.
* Begin the dialogue by coming up with a single statement of intent on what you are looking for - what are you trying to learn, for instance.
* Sigilize the statement.
* Write it on all the bills in your wallet/purse.
* Observe the bills that come to you, and the various occurrences in your life. Do you find any strange markings on the bills? Have there been any educational co-incidences?
* Continue to spend it as normal. As new bills come into your possession, put the sigil on them.
* If you find markings or writings on bills, sigilize them as well. Signal back that you're in a dialogue.
* If you feel your question/intent is answered, create a new statement, question, or response. Sigilize that and use that sigil.

Continue this exercise until you get the information or results you're seeking. Use the money as a vehicle to carry your requests and questions into the sphere of finances.

My experiments in this area worked well, but required definite dedication to almost constantly sigilizing your money and observation of what happens, but I found it useful to get to "know" the spirit of money. However, as an activity it definitely keeps you very aware of and in tune with your financial activities and what you're asking for. It also increases the attention you pay to money and your focus on it.

Closing

Using any or all of the four techniques above, I recommend you give the use of physical currency in your magic a try. I'd say more - but there's nothing more to say. Besides, time is money - though that is probably for another essay entirely.

Vince Stevens is an IT Project Manager and experimental mage who lives on the west coast of the United States. He has engaged in both his technical and magical interests for over twenty years in an admittedly erratic, if enjoyable manner. His major focus is the use of magical and psychological practices to develop a completely integrated, magical life. For recreation he plays video games, works on websites, and speaks on various issues.

Sustainable (and Self-Sustainable) Investment
By Lupa

By now I bet you've gotten some good ideas on how to increase your financial intake—or at least better manage what you already have. This may mean that you're thinking about what to do with the extra money you have.

I know a lot of folks who, upon receiving an extra wad of cash, either through a tax return, work bonus, or birthday gift, figure out what sort of expensive toys they can buy for themselves. They might get a bigger TV or stereo, go on a shopping spree, or take a nice long vacation. Unfortunately, once that short-term indulgence is gone, they're left in the same position they were before—same bills, debts, and other expenses that they had prior to their temporary increase.

Others, with a little more practical mindset, may take that money and use it to pay off some debts. This can, of course, reduce the amount of interest paid monthly and improve their credit scores. However, once again, when the money's gone, it's gone for good.

An option that is often overlooked is that of investment. Part of the reason is because, quite frankly, it's not the world's most riveting topic as far as most people are concerned. It takes a certain amount of education, formal or informal, to learn how to effectively watch and utilize the stock market. Good investments require meticulous bookkeeping, both to make sure you have the amount of money you think you do, and to assure correct tax filing. And let's face it "mutual funds", "Roth IRA" and "capital gain" aren't nearly as exciting to most people as "American Idol", "Ben and Jerry's", and "HBO".

The other reason some people, pagans and magicians included, may ignore the possibility of investing their money is the idea that this must necessarily feed evil, soulless corporations on Wall Street, lining the pockets of big-business fat cats, and contributing funds to everything from sweatshops to environmental destruction. This goes hand in hand with the knee jerk reaction that money is inherently bad and that the only people who want more than they need to survive are capitalist vampires feeding off a poor, underprivileged populace.

As you've probably read in other essays, though, money itself is like magic. It's a tool, neither inherently good nor evil. What is important is what the individual person does with that money.

Unfortunately, some people do choose to use it as a tool to screw over others. This doesn't mean that if you find yourself making more money than what is required for monthly bills you'll automatically turn into a selfish capitalist pig. You may have to pay more attention to your own needs and financial cycles, as well as the machinations of the economy on a larger scale, but ultimately what you do with your money is entirely up to you.

Why Invest?

How old are you right now? Now, how many years away are you from the age of retirement (we'll say sixty-five years old)? If you're about my age (twenty-nine as of this publication) sixty-five may seem a long time away. However, we're not immortal, at least not in the flesh. And as distasteful and/or inconvenient as it may seem, money is necessary to live almost everywhere. Even if you live on a commune, raising your own food, there are certain things that you need money for when dealing with the outside world.

So let's think about being sixty-five years old. You're probably not going to be quite as spry and flexible as you are now, especially if you're about my age. Your body will probably be achier, with more little quirks. Depending on your lifestyle, environment, genetics, and other factors, you may have a long-term condition to deal with, such as diabetes, which requires regular medicinal treatment. You might even end up with a disability at some point between now and then that makes it tougher, if not impossible, to work (and at least in the U.S. disability compensation isn't that great if you're not insured).

You're also going to have to decide when to stop working, at least on a full time basis. It may be easy now to say "Well, I'll just work til the day I die!". It may not be so simple when you're around retirement age. Do you like working now? Would you rather be out doing your own thing? You'll probably feel the same way later, if not more so. And once you stop working, that's it—no more paycheck. Nobody's going to pay your way for you, unless you have a financially secure and loving family who's willing to pay your bills. Even then, it's rather selfish to assume that they'll want to pay for your every need, and the luxuries may be few and far between, depending on the situation.

With the way social security in the U.S. is going, I highly doubt there's going to be anything left for me when I come of age. And from what I've heard, it's not an incredibly large payoff, either. So it's a bad idea for me to depend on the government to support me when I'm older. I'm also not going to depend on the pagan and occult communities to pay my way when things get tight. It's not that I don't love you people, but you've got your own issues to deal with. And having seen a few pagan elders struggling these days, I don't want to be in that situation myself a few decades from now.

Nor do I want to be the senior citizen standing at the front of ~~Wal~~ Hell-mart making minimum wage for greeting people while spending the entire day on my aching feet and knees. I sure as hell don't want to be sixty-five and working in a McDonald's with a manager a third my age telling me how to mop the damned floor. I don't trust our society to change the state of affairs, either. Senior citizens get a raw deal now, and I don't see it changing any time soon. I can work for social change, but given how much this culture resists reform, I'm not counting on a free ride four decades from now.

What this all leaves me with is the conclusion that I have to look after myself. I am responsible for me. I may have my pagan tribe that gives me social support, and helps me in tough situations—but is it really fair for me to just assume that someone else will cover my bills for me, or pay to repair my vehicle, or buy me the medicine I need to get better—or stay alive? When I hit sixty-five, if I'm not already self-employed or otherwise financially stable, I want to be able to stop working for someone else at that point and retire in peace. I don't want to have to live on dog food, either, and I'd like to travel and do other things that work kept me from doing. Since I don't have children and don't intend to have them (and wouldn't force them to care for me when I'm older, anyway), it's up to me to ensure I have a secure future.

And that means looking into investments.

Sustainable Investing

Remember earlier when I talked about the notion that all investments feed evil corporate entities? Well, that's not entirely true. There are numerous resources for investing in green companies and environmentally-friendly causes that can earn you a healthy return. At the same time you'll be giving less money to unethical companies, sweat shops, and polluters.

Before you invest, you're going to have to figure the amount of interest you owe on any debts you have. (If you don't have any, proceed on to the next paragraph—and know that I envy you!) The reason is that if the interest you're paying on debts is higher than the interest received in your investments, you're actually losing money over the long term. I would recommend reconfiguring your budget to maximize the amount of money you can put towards getting rid of debts while maintaining a nice financial cushion for emergencies in a savings account. Once you have the highest interest debts paid off and can reasonably make money investing, the next thing you want to determine is what sort of investments you want to make.

Sustainable Investing (www.sustainableinvesting.net) is a good starting place. The site offers information on both individual investments, as well as larger deals for professional investors. I'm going to assume that most of my audience here will be more interested in individual investments, so that's where I'll focus. The site features mutual funds and stocks, as well as information on green real estate, banks that support sustainable practices, carbon offsets, and other areas of interest.

Starting with the mutual funds, the portfolios offered vary in "green factor", so to speak. For example, the Sierra Club's holdings seem to run more toward conventional companies, such as Hewlett Packard, Apple Incorporated, and St. Jude Medical.[27] The Winslow Green Growth portfolio includes investments in Whole Foods, Wild Oats, and Green Mountain Coffee Roasters.[28] Therefore, don't assume that everything that's labeled "sustainable" will be equal. Sustainable Investing and the Yahoo! Finance sites that it links to clearly outline the holdings of the various portfolios so it's easy to do research on each portfolio.

Their page of stocks is similarly well-organized. Over 100 stocks are listed, along with the reason why they're considered sustainable. The reasons range from what the company works with (alternative energy, recycling) to good or improved environmental and related policies. Some of the companies found in the mutual fund holdings may be investigated further here. For example, Hewlett Packard is on the list of sustainable stocks because of its policies. You can then use the information provided with both the stocks and mutual funds to find out what companies you wish to support.

Sustainable Investing is just one of many resources available to you. If you google "sustainable investing" you'll get plenty of websites. Sustainable Business (www.sustainablebusiness.com) has a general news site for sustainable investment and other business practices that also features *The Progressive Investor* magazine. You can get affordable financial advice, including on investments, at First Sustainable

---

[27] http://finance.yahoo.com/q/hl?s=SCFSX, 4 August
[28] http://finance.yahoo.com/q/hl?s=WGGFX, 4 August

(www.firstsustainable.com). Resources aren't limited to the U.S., either. Sirius (www.sirius.com.au) is based in Melbourne, Australia, while Asria (www.asria.org) focuses on the Asian Pacific region. Take your time, read as much as you can, and find other people to talk to about financial planning. This includes not only professionals, but friends and family members who may be wellsprings of information (whether you expected it or not!).

If you're already experienced in investing, it's a simple matter at this point to figure out what sorts of risks and returns are best for your situation. If this is all new to you, on the other hand, I highly suggest doing research on basic investing. *The Motley Fool Investment Guide* by David and Tom Gardner, as well as their website (www.fool.com) are excellent resources. If you're in a long term relationship, David Bach's *Smart Couples Finish Rich* is also an invaluable guide. You don't necessarily have to have an expensive stock broker do all the work for you, but it is important to have a basic understanding of how investments work and how to determine what's best for your personal situation before investing your money.

Magic and Investments

While money is very much a mundane, earthy subject in a lot of ways, investing it can be used in magic as well. For example, part of my offering to the totem animals I work with involves giving some of my money to help their physical children. A portion of the money that I make from my artwork and writing is given to the Defenders of Wildlife (www.defenders.org) as a donation. This helps the Defenders in their campaigns to help preserve habitat and strengthen reintroduction programs for large predators and other animals. Once I have my investments in order I intend to draw a certain amount from what is made to add to that donation.

To that end, the money that is initially invested may be blessed before being sent off to the company managing your investments. This may take the form of a paper check or money order, though in this day and age you may simply use plastic and your computer. Either way, you can bring the paraphernalia of investing into your ritual area. Bless and/or charge the money (or the representation thereof) that will be invested with the intent that it will help not only you but the spirits/entities/causes of your choice. You may ask various entities for help increasing the return for maximum effect.

In fact, you might even seek out a deity or other entity associated with money to help you with your investments. You can also create a servitor for this purpose if there's not a preexisting entity that you think can help. While the entity shouldn't replace your broker or other sources, s/he may be able to help bring opportunities your way or alert you to good possible investments. Make sure your intention is clear, that you want to invest in something that not only has a good return, but also has sustainable business practices.

If You Can't Play the Stocks Right Now...

Investing can be expensive. Some investments may require a minimum initial amount that's more than what you have available at the time. Or you may still be stuck in enough debt that it's not profitable to invest until those debts are out of the way. In the meantime, you can still help make a difference with your dollars.

For example, when I lived in Pittsburgh, PA, most of the electricity in my home came from coal power plants. So I signed up with Green Mountain Energy (www.greenmountainenergy.com) and had a portion of my electricity diverted from coal to renewable resources such as wind energy. The options vary from state to state (Green Mountain no longer has services in Pennsylvania), but in many states you can opt to have some or even all of your energy come from renewable sources.

Buying products made from recycled and other sustainable materials is another excellent way of giving money to green companies. In many places toilet paper made from recycled paper (including a large percentage of post-consumer waste) is only a small amount more expensive than conventional, tree-based, chlorine bleached toilet paper. Most office supply stores, including chain stores, carry recycled office paper. Small independent shops carry gifts and clothing made of reclaimed or sweatshop free components. Some cities even have companies that salvage leftover or used hardware and building supplies and sell them at a deep discount to DIYers.

Organic produce and free range meat are still more expensive than conventional food, but even adding one or two items to your grocery list per week can help, and won't be too much strain on your wallet. Better yet, if you have a local farmer's market, you can find out exactly how your food was produced, and you cut down on the resources used to transport your food from the farm to your home. And you give back to the local economy and individual people instead of huge corporations; considering the number of farmers who require government subsidies to get by, this can make a huge difference.

Being more conscious in your shopping choices is another way of investing in sustainable companies. It may not get those companies as much money as buying their stocks (if available) but it is a way of making your money count for more. And once you do get to the point where you can invest, you can also continue in your sustainable shopping practices.

Lupa is a pagan and experimental magician living in Portland, OR with hir mate and fellow author, Taylor Ellwood. S/he is owned by Sun Ce and Ember the cats, and shares hir home with too many books and art supplies. Lupa is the author of *Fang and Fur, Blood and Bone: A Primal Guide to Animal Magic*, *A Field Guide to Otherkin*, *Kink Magic: Sex Magic Beyond Vanilla* (cowritten with Ellwood) and is a contributor to the *Magick on the Edge* anthology. S/he is currently editing *Talking About the Elephant: An Anthology of Neopagan Perspectives on Cultural Appropriation.*(Autumn 2008) Hir current solo book projects include *DIY Totemism: Your Personal Guide to Animal Totems* (Autumn 2008) and an as-of-yet untitled sequel to *A Field Guide to Otherkin*. S/he can be found online at http://www.thegreenwolf.com.

Did You Like What You Read?

Inner Alchemy by Taylor Ellwood
ISBN 978-1-905713-06-6/MB0106
$21.99/£12.99 paperback
Neurotransmitter spirit guides, DNA magic, energy work, and other topics on the magic within your own body.

Ogam: Weaving Word Wisdom by Erynn Rowan Laurie
ISBN 978-1-905713-02-8/MB0110
$22.49/£12.99 paperback

Based on the author's years of experience with ogam, this text provides the most complete guide to the ancient Celtic divination/magical system.

Magick on the Edge edited by Taylor Ellwood
ISBN 978-1-905713-05-3/MB0105
$22.49/£12.99 paperback
An anthology featuring experimental magical practices from over 20 experienced, innovative magicians on everything from time magic to the art of magical graffiti to sex magic and more!

Graeco-Egyptian Magick by Tony Mierzwicki
ISBN 978-1-905713-03-7/MB0103
$21.99/£12.99 paperback
The recreation of a planetary system of self-initiation using authentic Graeco-Egyptian Magick, as practiced in Egypt during the first five centuries CE. Drawn from sources contemporary to the first hermetic magicians.

Find these and the rest of our current lineup at http://www.immanion-press.com

Breinigsville, PA USA
01 October 2009
225127BV00001B/3/P